MASTERING
CHURCH
FINANCES

Richard L. Bergstrom
Gary Fenton
Wayne A. Pohl

MULTNOMAH

Portland, Oregon 97266

Christianity Today, Inc.

MASTERING CHURCH FINANCES
© 1992 by Christianity Today, Inc.
Published by Multnomah Press
Portland, Oregon 97266

Multnomah Press is a ministry of
Multnomah School of the Bible
8435 NE Glisan Street
Portland, Oregon 97220

Printed in the United States of America.

Library of Congress Cataloging-in-Publication Data

Bergstrom, Richard L.
    Mastering church finances / Richard L. Bergstrom, Gary Fenton, Wayne A. Pohl.
        p. cm. — (mastering ministry)
        ISBN 0-88070-506-X
        1. Church finance. I. Fenton, Gary. II. Pohl, Wayne A. III. Title.
IV. Series.
BV770.B47   1992
254.8—dc20   92-9547
                                      CIP

94 95 96 97 98 99 - 10 9 8 7 6 5 4 3 2

Contents

Introduction   7
Craig Brian Larson

Part 1
Setting the Atmosphere

1. How Your Church Feels About Money   13
   Gary Fenton

2. Can Finance People Be Ministry Minded?   29
   Richard Bergstrom

3. The Spiritual Side of Mammon   41
   Wayne Pohl

4. The Moneywise Pastor   51
   Gary Fenton

Part 2
Raising and Monitoring Money

5. Developing Generous Givers   65
   Wayne Pohl

6. How to Handle Designated Funds   75
   Gary Fenton

7. Ministry to Deep-Pocket Donors   87
   Wayne Pohl

8. Where Churches Are Vulnerable   99
   Richard Bergstrom

9. Insuring Financial Integrity   115
   Richard Bergstrom

Part 3
Spending and Investing Money

10. Determining Which Ministry Gets What   129
    Gary Fenton

11. Who Spends the Church's Money?   141
    Richard Bergstrom

12. Setting Staff Salaries   153
    Wayne Pohl

   Epilogue   165
   Craig Brian Larson

Introduction

When I began ministry as an associate, my pastor charged me with two duties that soon bore hard: counting Sunday's offering and posting donors' contributions to tax records.

I did my job but without enthusiasm. In my mind these duties were unspiritual. They distracted from real ministry: namely Bible study and prayer, message preparation and discipleship. Looking to the example of the apostles in Acts 6, I thought these two financial tasks should be carried by someone else. I knew money was necessary (after all, I did appreciate my paycheck), but I didn't personally want to bother with it.

I got a different perspective on money, however, a few years later. As a pastor in the process of preaching through the Gospel of Luke, I came upon the parable of the shrewd manager, in chapter 16, whose savvy with money kept a roof over his head after he had been fired by his master. For the first time, Christ's explanation of the story hit me squarely: "Whoever can be trusted with very little can also be trusted with much, and whoever is dishonest with very little will also be dishonest with much. So if you have not been trustworthy in handling worldly wealth, who will trust you with true riches? And if you have not been trustworthy with someone else's property, who will give you property of your own?"

I realized that in God's eyes managing money was not a distraction from real ministry but a proving ground for real ministry. By handling financial responsibilities well, I showed myself capable of handling spiritual responsibilities well.

That didn't mean that as pastor I had to pencil in all the numbers on the monthly expense journal, but I did have to ensure it was done right, on time, and according to our denomination's standards. Ours being a small church with volunteer office help, that was often a challenge.

As the shrewd-manager parable shows, church financial management is a worthy test. At times, in fact, it resembles an obstacle course, studded with lean budgets, differing expectations, designated offerings, shaky internal control, rotating treasurers, reluctant offering counters, hair-raising annual business meetings (where friendly fire takes on new meaning), and daunting building programs. In such a proving ground, how easy it is for even well-meaning ministers to break their ankles.

The obstacle course of church finances, fortunately, can be navigated, and for this volume of Mastering Ministry we've brought together three authors who have successfully done so.

Richard Bergstrom

Richard would rather not have earned some of his financial stripes. A few months after becoming pastor of Euzoa Bible Church in Steamboat Springs, Colorado, he discovered the church's youth pastor had been embezzling funds, nearly $42,000 over a period of six years. He confronted the man and the situation, leading the church through the crisis, and revamping the church's internal control systems to ensure financial integrity.

The watchwords undergirding sound financial practices are expressed by Richard this way, "No system is beyond abuse, but responsible stewardship demands church finances be handled with absolute integrity."

The measures Bergstrom instituted were successful: "As a result of aggressive reform and complete openness before our church body, the level of stewardship did not decline but rather increased after the embezzlement problem had been cleared up."

Before coming to Euzoa Bible Church, Richard served as pastor of Samish Way Baptist Church in Bellingham, Washington, where he led the church through a building project.

Richard is currently serving as director of the northwest division of Church Dynamics International, a church consulting ministry, where he uses his experience to help other churches establish steady spiritual and financial bases. He has earned a doctor of ministry degree from Western Conservative Baptist Seminary in Portland, Oregon, and a master of divinity from Denver Seminary in Colorado.

Gary Fenton

Gary knows church finances are not an absolute science: "It's not enough to manage the finances according to 'sound business principles,' because the definition of 'sound business principles' varies widely, shaped by the culture, mindset, and financial setting of each particular community."

That is spoken like a man whose hands have gotten greasy in the gearbox of the church. Fenton has ratcheted the bolts in six pastorates, ranging from an agricultural area to a community with a highly competitive tourist industry, from a university community to a small city dependent on the oil industry. He now pastors Dawson Memorial Baptist Church in Birmingham, Alabama.

Gary manages to combine a tough-minded approach to church finances and church politics with a tenderhearted concern for the spiritual health of a congregation.

He has earned a doctor of ministry degree from Midwestern Baptist Theological Seminary in Kansas City, Missouri, and a master of divinity degree from Southwestern Baptist Theological Seminary in Fort Worth, Texas.

Wayne Pohl

As we sat around the conference table talking about finances, I noticed something about Wayne Pohl: over a period of several hours he never sat back in his chair. In conversation, he leans forward, looks you right in the eye, talks in a strong voice, and answers questions with assurance. You get the feeling that the dollars are under control at St. Paul's Lutheran Church in Trenton, Michigan.

Wayne Pohl believes that giving patterns reveal as much about a Christian and a church as anything. On any Monday morning he can boot up his computer, call a confidential file, and read what each of the over 1,000 church attenders donated the previous day. He is a pastor, and those numbers are a spiritual barometer.

During his nearly two decades as pastor of St. Paul's, Wayne has led the church through numerical growth, financial growth, and two building programs. Previously he served as mission developer and pastor of St. Mark Lutheran Church in Kentwood, Michigan. He earned his master of divinity degree from Concordia Seminary.

Whether yours is a one-offering-plate church or a one-Brinks-truck-to-the-bank church, these pastors have loads to say about how to best strengthen and manage its finances. We are confident that their advice will make your proving ground significantly less menacing and more focused on ministry.

— *Craig Brian Larson*
associate editor, LEADERSHIP
Carol Stream, Illinois

Part One
Setting the
Atmosphere

It's not enough to manage church finances according to "sound business principles," because the definition of "sound business principles" varies widely, shaped by the culture, mindset, and financial setting of each particular community.

— Gary Fenton

CHAPTER ONE

How Your Church Feels About Money

Late one evening, a young pastor called me, a frantic tone in his voice. He quickly got to the point: he feared he was about to be fired.

He outlined his story. Nine months earlier, when he accepted the church's invitation to become pastor, the church's needs and his gifts had seemed a good match.

Although the church had a budget, the former pastors and treasurer had never followed it. Upon the death of the tenured treasurer and the resignation of the pastor at about that same time, the church thought it a good time to bring order to their financial chaos.

According to the pulpit committee, the church needed a pastor with administrative gifts; according to this young pastor's own understanding and the evaluation of his peers, administration was his strength.

My friend quickly applied some of his organizational skills and set up a new structure for managing the money. Because his new system gave more responsibility to people and less control to the pastor, he assumed his new semi-rural, conservative parishioners would rise up and call him blessed.

Instead, they rose up and blasted him.

The same leaders who had wanted him because of his management skills were criticizing him publicly for lack of administrative ability. The leaders felt they had been misled.

The pastor, for his part, felt betrayed. He counterpunched by reminding the leaders of the church's financial chaos when he began. One long-time church leader said he preferred chaos to the new system. Soon the pastor and leaders were questioning each other's integrity.

What went wrong? Did the pastor lack financial and organizational skills? Did the lay leadership overestimate their management abilities? Or was something else at work here?

Although many factors can cause pastor-versus-church conflicts, money issues are likely near the top of the list. After visiting the church and hearing both sides, I became convinced that neither the pastor nor the lay leaders were inept or lacking in integrity. The pastor simply followed business principles used in a large corporation, and the church leadership followed principles used in small, privately owned farms and businesses.

It's not enough to manage the finances according to "sound business principles," because the definition of "sound business principles" varies widely, shaped by the culture, mindset, and financial setting of each particular community.

I have served churches in four settings: an agricultural area, a community with a highly competitive tourist industry, a university community, and a small city dependent on the oil industry. Each church's financial accounting system reflected, in different degrees, the local community's prevailing definition of good business.

I've also visited with other pastors and churches, and I've supervised a number of doctoral students serving as pastors. I've found at least five models of financial management used in communities and churches. By no means is my list comprehensive, but recognizing the differences between these five has helped me and others manage our churches' financial affairs.

The Family-Business Church — Lovers of Thrift

Many smaller communities operate on family-owned business economies. This is especially true in agricultural areas. Farms are family-owned businesses, and often the small town nearby is dominated by family-owned enterprises: the car dealership, the Dairy Queen, the service station, and the clothing store.

In family-owned businesses, the owner knows every cost and expenditure. He or she knows the price of raw materials, utilities, labor, and even the paper towels in the restrooms. The owner or manager knows that if he loses touch with costs, he will likely lose the business. So, knowing the details becomes a prized principle of good business.

The survival of the family-owned business often depends on its ability to serve customers well. Since the owner is usually responsible for the quality of service, he or she personally seeks to discover the needs of customers and listens to their complaints.

In the family-owned business culture, the pastor of a local church is often viewed as the business manager of the church, expected to know the cost of each and every item the church purchases. In such a church, "sound business principles" mean that the pastor is knowledgeable about financial details.

In one church I served, I heard (frequently) about a former pastor who discouraged a committee, which was shopping for a church lawn mower, from taking bids from *every* local store. The committee had obtained prices from all but one local distributor, and according to the oft told legend, the pastor told them not to waste their time with the other merchant.

After the committee purchased the lawn mower, the chairman discovered the church could have saved nearly ten dollars on the two–hundred dollar purchase from the other distributor. This story (and embellished versions of it) was rehearsed many times by the men of this small church to illustrate the irresponsibility of the former pastor.

The issue was not so much the ten dollars but that the pastor did not handle the purchase as the owner of a small business usually does. Consequently, the pastor couldn't get the church to enact some of his programs, and during my pastorate he was still remembered as an extravagant spender, even though his purchases often expedited programs.

In the family-business church, then, thrift is the highest virtue. Thriftiness may not produce change, but it keeps disaster at bay. The pastor may convince a congregation not to worship thrift but will probably never convince it to abandon thrift as a primary principle of management.

This does not mean, though, that the pastor must be involved in the purchase of every item. Several years ago I led revival services in a church located in a town of less than 5,000 people. The church had been served by the same pastor for ten years. Several times during that week, members told me their pastor was not only a great preacher and pastor but also a good business manager.

That surprised me, because he didn't seem consumed by the church's financial details. I asked him why people thought of him in this way.

"Early in my ministry here," he replied, "I found people continually asking me about expenditures, and I was continually replying, 'I don't know.' Some of the old timers felt I was unconcerned about administration. As a result, I asked the treasurer and the secretary to provide me a list each month of all the checks written and what products or services the checks had purchased. Prior to each business conference, I began spending an hour reviewing the list. Consequently in the business conferences, I never appeared surprised at people's questions."

He concluded, "These have been the best hours I've spent for saving me time and bringing me credibility."

In such churches, the committees and boards responsible for church business often bog down discussing small expenditures. Many pastors are tempted to accelerate the discussion or even bypass it altogether. But such pastors risk being seen as poor stewards, since they don't seem concerned about the smallest expenditures.

The pastor of a family-business church is also seen as the primary provider of services, much like the owner of a small business. The provider of services, of course, must listen to the complaints of the clients.

Among other things, the pastor in this setting must listen to complaints about spending. If someone complains that the church is paying too much for light bulbs, the pastor will need to graciously listen to these comments instead of telling the meter watcher to take the matter up with the buildings and grounds chairman.

As pastors, we can slowly educate people to ask such questions of others, but to ignore those questions is to ask for small-business churches to question your management and integrity.

The Entrepreneurial Church — Risk Takers

A second type of church with distinct financial characteristics is the entrepreneurial church. Often this spirit is found in towns where prominent individuals have started their first business.

In contrast to family-owned businesses, many of which are inherited, the businesses of entrepreneurs have been started from scratch. The family-owned businessman may practice thrift to preserve what he has; the entrepreneur is striving to build a business and create a profit through calculated indebtedness.

The entrepreneur is, then, a risk taker. And entrepreneurs view risk taking as a sign of character. These types often gather and swap risk-taking stories the way self-help group leaders tell pain stories.

Translated into church language, financial risk taking is seen as evidence of spirituality. Such people may think the pastor who refuses to risk lacks faith.

Most ministers advocate the value of moving out on faith, but many are wary of risking their own financial future and career, and for good reason. But leaders in an entrepreneurial church live in a world where bankruptcy is a constant threat. Some of them live on the edge of financial collapse each time they print out a new spread sheet. They have little sympathy for a pastor who calls the church to risk but then is unwilling to risk anything personally.

During the high oil prices of the early 1980s, one entrepreneurial church in a booming suburb considered making the compensation of the staff entirely performance related. The pastor reacted so vehemently against the idea that his leadership was challenged, his credibility disappeared, and he soon left.

The new pastor negotiated the issue, explaining the disadvantages of the plan. At the same time, he didn't seek to have every benefit and perk guaranteed.

Later, one of that church's key lay leaders told me the church thought that the new pastor was "a man of faith" and that the previous pastor had failed to practice what he preached.

Entrepreneurial communities honor effectiveness more than thriftiness. Entrepreneurs want results. The entrepreneur is willing to lose money if he feels the potential of gain is worth the risk. Entrepreneurs describe their work in terms of how much they make rather than how much they save.

My first encounter with this culture occurred while pastoring in an emerging tourist town. I was surprised at the ease with which we spent money, for we were not a wealthy church.

One time I made a rather passionate plea to a committee to fund a summer program to bring students in to do ministry among tourists. Much to my surprise, the committee doubled my request for funds. The project succeeded, and no one objected to the fact that the same results could have been accomplished with much less money.

Other projects more worthwhile (like badly needed building repairs) suffered for lack of funding, but this particular project became sacred because it was measurably effective.

Entrepreneurial people are goal oriented, and they bring that orientation with them to church. But their goals usually include money. So the pastor whose goals and vision for the church exclude financial concerns may have trouble gaining a following for *ministry* ideas.

In the entrepreneurial church I served, I arrived with goals for church growth, and soon I developed these into specific program goals. I presented the master plan to the deacons, and they endorsed it, though without much enthusiasm.

I was disappointed by their calm response, because I had hoped my plan would spark discussion. I wanted their input, but they accepted the goals with little excitement.

My enthusiasm for the plan carried me through my first fifteen months there. Finally, though, one of the men in the church challenged me to set not only goals for church membership but also financial goals (like projecting the church's budget two and three years ahead and determining how much could be set aside for a new building).

I thought focusing attention on finances was "unspiritual." I saw money as a means and not the end. Setting money goals smacked of materialism.

Nonetheless, I reluctantly prepared some financial goals and took them to the appropriate groups. I was surprised to see that these financial goals became the catalyst for the discussion I had hoped for earlier. We met three times within one month, and I was able to use the "means" goals to discuss the "end" goals.

Setting the financial goals provided the opportunity among these entrepreneurs for vision setting and vision selling. This group then completely reworked, revised, and improved the master plan.

Entrepreneurial churches appear to change pastors and staff members with great ease. The grief process after a resignation or termination does not appear to be as long as in other churches. In the world of the entrepreneur, leadership changes are common.

Pastors who feel their emotional world would collapse by being dismissed probably will not be able to function in this type of economic setting. As one business executive, speaking about a friend in the ministry, told me, "He would be a much better pastor if he didn't think termination was terminal."

In entrepreneurial churches, financial plans are constantly being revised. They function in a world where financial structures change dramatically.

I once lived in a community in which three of the four largest banks changed ownership and philosophy in a four-year period. The largest bank had four names and three different corporate owners and had added two new branches in five years. And we were not the exception in the Southwest.

That impacts the local church. A pastor who serves a church located in a yuppie suburb told me, tongue in cheek, "My church expects a new five-year plan every eighteen months."

This is an exciting type of church in which to serve, but there is an inherent weakness in this financial atmosphere. Sometimes, in pursuit of results, efficiency is undervalued and even despised. Thus, the church may suddenly find itself in financial problems.

Furthermore, successful entrepreneurs, programmed to cut their losses, may decide to leave the church they've decided has no future. Stability is not valued in this type of church, unless it's simply a stage on the way to becoming a super church.

I once met with a church that in its previous twelve years had fired three of its four pastors. During this same period, this church also had built three new buildings, received the denomination's distinction of being "the fastest growing church in the state" two different years, and gone through a bitter split. The attendance for the adult morning Bible study during this twelve-year period had been as high as five hundred but had dropped to less than two hundred. According to a denominational worker, most of their problems related to finances.

Some of the reasons for this lack of stability I discovered as I learned about the community. Most cities have several suburban rings that usually correlate to social and economic groupings. This community was located on the second outer ring of a progressive city. These folks were young riskers who had purchased small acreages in a nearby community that real estate people were suggesting would explode in residential growth. These young bucks had told their wives and children they were buying into semi-rural living, but they were really trying to buy futures in the real estate market.

Only one of the four pastors in the last twelve years had been entrepreneurial, and unfortunately he had been a high risk taker in his marriage and lost his position due to immorality.

The next pastor wanted to bring stability by removing risk from the church's financial program, but his low-risk style alienated some families from the church. He was fired, and the charges against him included a "lack of vision."

The church has now called a pastor who takes calculated risks. He's seen not as a caretaker but as a man of vision. His vision is carefully thought through, though, and the church's attendance is on the increase.

The Nonprofit Community — Lovers of Process

A significant number of our communities are dominated by nonprofit organizations such as government entities, universities, and religious bodies.

People with experience in nonprofits have a different value system and vocabulary than do entrepreneurs and small-business owners.

A pastor moved to a bedroom community close to a state capital. Most of the members worked for the state government or for a government-funded agency. The pastor had assumed that since the community was relatively small, the management principles he had mastered in the other small town in which he had pastored would transfer. But within three months he was in deep trouble with the lay leaders.

At an area conference, this pastor told me he was aggressively seeking another church. He was used to informally supervising staff, without resorting to formal job descriptions. But people would regularly ask him upon what basis he delegated duties.

Others would question him about money management.

Finance committee meetings consumed over three hours as members dissected the church's finances. All this left him angry, confused, and believing his integrity was challenged.

When I moved to a university community, an older pastor gave me some wise advice: "If you will accept questions as compliments or as requests for your approval, you will love working with university professors. If you see their questions as threats or delays, you will be miserable."

Most nonprofit organizations create energy through study and analysis, and that means asking lots of questions. If a young professor on a university campus wishes to impress her department head, she poses the difficult, intriguing question in a faculty meeting. Good questions are rewarded in the academic setting, and often the person asking the question is a committed team player.

Most nonprofits are most closely modeled after the academic community (although some nonprofits are beginning to model themselves on an entrepreneurial model).

A minister of education with an impressive resume and list of achievements asked me to help him relocate. He indicated that, because of church tensions, his pastor and most of the staff were looking for places to serve as well.

"What are the reasons for the tension?" I asked.

He said that everything the pastor and staff did was questioned. He mentioned by name one woman in particular who pestered him, asking before each decision how it would relate to the mission statement of the church. She served on the church's finance committee and continually examined his budget, even asking for written self-evaluations on some of his programs.

I had served with this woman on a local community board and found her to be a caring and articulate Ph.D. She asked the same kind of questions in our board meetings even though she and the executive director of this agency were close friends. I am convinced that she saw this as her way of fulfilling her duties both on the board and in the church.

Members of nonprofit communities do not see committee meetings and business conferences as perfunctory. While serving in a church dominated by the university community, I found that business committees could devote forty minutes to a single, seemingly minute issue. Questions would be asked and recommendations made regarding the slightest detail.

Often I noticed new members become tense in this process. They seemed afraid that a verbal explosion was imminent, only to discover that when we finally voted, we had either unanimous or overwhelming majority approval.

Study, of course, can become an end in itself. My greatest frustration in the nonprofit church I served was the large number of ad hoc study committees that were continually at work.

One staff member told me he thought *ad hoc* was Latin for "to slow down" because that was the primary function performed by many of these temporary, single-issue committees.

In the world where these people live, though, study committees are a part of good and necessary management. Nonprofits live off of the voluntary generosity or the taxes of others, and as a result they feel an obligation to avoid failure. Most pastors see the resources as belonging to the Lord, and we may not be as sensitive to the donor as people in other nonprofits.

Another trait: nonprofits are primarily print-oriented organizations. Printed reports are the primary means of telling supporters, clients, and constituents what is happening. As a result, motions and recommendations need to be worded carefully. Print is more precise than spoken reports, and an effective leader of nonprofits learns to word his or her recommendations in print clearly and accurately.

I have seen a finance committee vote to spend $70,000 to repair a church-owned building and then appoint a special committee, giving them two weeks to properly word the motion before presenting it to the church.

One committee member, relatively new to this particular church, ridiculed the committee for wasting time. He had just moved to town and purchased a fast–food franchise quicker than they could word a statement. Members of the committee, to this day, question this man's stability, even though his annual income now surpasses any three of the professors on the committee.

Finally, in nonprofits, *process* is as important as *results*. Nonprofits generally attract people committed to principles more than product. This may be changing as the entrepreneurial types move into leadership of nonprofits, but I think most nonprofits' employees are not primarily interested in the bottom line.

It is assumed, for instance, that the person charged with supervising finances and spending money will follow procedures, even if the organization suffers as a result. To violate the process is to violate the group, even if the group benefits from expediency.

A pastor who served a church with a large number of government employees told me that he and the newly elected church treasurer once moved some church funds from one financial institution to another, doing so without checking with the entire finance committee. It was an emergency situation, and their actions saved the church well over $3,000.

When he and the treasurer reported this to the finance committee, they expected the committee to congratulate them on their wisdom. Instead, they were openly criticized. The saving of $3,000 proved to be costly to this pastor's credibility, which took two years to reestablish.

The Corporate Setting — Competitors for Approval

A fourth environment in which churches operate is the corporate setting. Some communities are dominated by people who work for large corporations.

Generally, people in corporations have specialized views on money; some are trained to create new money through sales and user fees; others are trained to save money by financial control. Few people in a corporation are trained to see the big picture.

Since senior management — the big–picture people — have to say no to many departments' requests, they are the most resented in the company. On the other hand, those who are trained to become specialists often have difficulty becoming big-picture people.

In a church of this culture, the pastor may be seen as the big-picture person, the one to whom members must bring their specific interests for evaluation and blessing. Although a church in a corporate community may be committee driven, many of the key members will probably assume that their special interests ultimately need the pastor's blessing to be implemented.

The Christian education committee, the missions committee, and the music committee become competing interests, each crusading for more resources. If the pastor rejects their ideas, people may become angry — until, that is, they have another idea that needs approval. If their report is accepted, they see the pastor as an ally — until, that is, the time when their proposal fails.

Pastors who have been most successful in this system accept the necessity of adversarial relationships. In a corporation, competition between individuals can build strong products. The tension is accepted as a necessary part of creativity.

But many pastors, including myself, have difficulty working with even temporary adversaries. I tend to believe people are either for or against me personally.

Recently one well-known pastor publicly prayed that God would forgive those who disagreed with him. We may feel like doing that, but it limits our effectiveness in the corporate culture.

Also, most corporations have a clearly defined chain of command for making decisions, spending money, and allocating resources. Some points on the chain are perfunctory stops, although corporate workers know they must make every stop. But they also know that each stop is not equal. The effective corporate climber knows where to make full stops and where to make whistle stops.

The pastor and staff can build credibility and become effective planners in the corporate church only by doing the same. In one church I've worked with, three committees had to be consulted before any major expenditure could be made: the finance committee, the planning committee, and the deacons.

The deacons were a whistle stop. When you mentioned to them the project that needed funding, they would rarely discuss it thoroughly before approving it. They just wanted to know what was going on. Woe to the person who tried to get something funded without informing the deacons!

On the other hand, the finance committee was a full stop. They had a major say in determining any spending, and they wanted to go over every proposal thoroughly. You figured to spend some time at this stop if you wanted a project funded.

The Mixed-Economy Church

Many churches have members from more than one of the above categories. This creates its own set of problems. In order to avoid misunderstanding, the pastor in this type of church may need to spend more time getting to know the lay leaders responsible for directing and evaluating the financial concerns of the church.

I once served a church in which the chairman of the finance committee was the primary spokesman about the congregation's finances. This position rotated annually, and in one three-year period it had been held, in turn, by a lawyer, a stockbroker, and an executive in an oil-related industry.

The committee rotated a third of its members each year, and at one point we had two real estate agents, two government employees, one man who started his own company, one hourly-wage employee, two attorneys, a homemaker, and a man who inherited his father's small business.

Helping this diverse group agree on good management procedures was no small challenge. I followed a pastor who had served this church for more than thirty years. After his retirement, he told me he had found that many of the conflicts on the finance committee were the result of the clash of the economic subcultures.

Consequently, when he was pastor, each January he visited each member of the finance committee. During his visit he found out what financial terms and phrases that person used in his or her business. He felt his major role in that committee was interpreting various financial tongues, helping the members communicate with one another.

Looking back on my first year as pastor at that church, I contributed to a volatile situation in the finance committee because I failed to see the diversity of the church. I assumed that all of the committee members were on the same page and made remarks to the committee that were misunderstood by some. As a result I spent more time explaining what I meant than it would have taken to get acquainted with our committee members in the first place.

Churches with highly diverse membership, and thus with highly diverse financial standards, may need to include interpretation as a regular agenda item at the annual leadership retreat.

Obvious forms of evil such as manipulation, lack of personal integrity, and misuse of funds are wrong in any kind of church. But many of the means we use to measure the quality of church business practices are finally subjective.

Furthermore, the flexibility needed to minister in many churches is not the result of lack of conviction but an honorable and necessary trait for successful financial management.

My goal is to lead people to become a family of faith. Recognizing that different churches approach financial management differently has not resolved all financial conflicts, but it has reduced these conflicts to a minimum. And that, in turn, makes it a lot easier to become a church family.

*If you want the finance committee to be ministry minded,
you need to recruit people who are on the front lines of
ministry themselves.*

— Richard L. Bergstrom

CHAPTER TWO

Can Finance People Be Ministry Minded?

After beginning the meeting with prayer, Don, the chairman of the finance committee, said, "I trust that all of you have had a chance to look over your copy of last year's budget."

"I'm afraid I didn't get mine," replied Dolores Anderson, the treasurer.

"Nor did I," added Pete. "Were they mailed out by the church office, Pastor?"

"Not to my knowledge," groaned Pastor Peterson. *Why does everybody always look at me when other people fail to do what they're supposed to do?* he thought to himself. "I guess the secretary neglected to get those out last week. I was hoping we'd be able to give some thought to this before our meeting tonight." He hated passing the buck like that, but at least the monkey was off his back.

"I'm sure we can go ahead with this tonight, Pastor," replied Don. "Dolores, will you please distribute copies of our financial report from the past eleven months. That will give us a guide to determine next year's budget. You'll notice, folks, that we were a little behind in our giving over the summer months. Our actual giving was 17 percent under the projected receipts. Fortunately, we were able to cut back in some areas over the summer so that we suffered an actual shortfall of only 4 percent. That leaves us with just $1,300 in the general fund as we enter the last month of our fiscal year."

"Pastor, I told you that budget was too ambitious," offered Ted, a retired teacher. "We need to be more conservative with how we spend the Lord's money."

"What about the endowment fund that was set up by Fred Bostrom's widow?" queried Lois, the financial secretary. "It seems a shame to have to cut back on important ministries with all that money sitting in the bank. Couldn't we at least use some of it to pay outstanding bills?"

"There is $125,000 in that fund," answered Don. "But I'm afraid we're not authorized to use that for anything other than the remodeling of the church sanctuary. That was the purpose designated by Mrs. Bostrom when she gave the gift. Unfortunately, that was five years ago. I know it has been three years since Edith's death, but it still would be a very sensitive issue to bring up to the family."

"I think we can get along just fine with the sanctuary as it is," chimed Peter Maxwell. "We need to increase our giving to missionaries. They haven't had a raise in five years."

If 'Max' had his way, thought Pastor Peterson, *he'd send all our money overseas — and I'd never get an associate. It doesn't look good for springing that one on the committee this year.*

"I'd recommend we hold off introducing any new ministries

for the next year," Don suggested. "In fact, it would appear to me that we need to make an across-the-board cut of 3 percent just to match our projected income over the next twelve months."

After a few minutes of discussion, Don asked, "All in favor of a 3-percent cut say, 'Aye.' "

"Aye."

"Unless there is other business, meeting adjourned."

I wish this were a complete fabrication. Unfortunately, it is a composite account of the way many church finance committees approach the financial planning process.

Why do committees so often act in a way that seems indifferent to and sometimes impedes ministry? The following practices may explain much of the problem:

— People making financial decisions are removed from first-hand involvement in ministry.

— People who are actually involved in the ministries have little or no input into the budget process.

— Little advance planning is put into the budget process.

— The focus is on the bottom line: How much did we take in? How much did we spend?

— Budget categories from previous years tend to dictate how money will be spent in subsequent years.

— The arrangement of the budget reflects an emphasis on maintaining a physical plant and paying staff salaries rather than fulfilling a corporate vision.

How can we avoid this approach? How can we move beyond seeing church ministry only in terms of budget numbers?

Staff the Finance Committee with Those Active in Ministry

When nominating committees consider candidates for the finance committee, they first look, and not without reason, to bankers, CPA's, and successful business people. Financial expertise is the first prerequisite, not involvement in ministry.

If you want the finance committee to be ministry minded,

though, you need to recruit people who are on the front lines of ministry themselves. Only people involved in ministry are going to be ministry minded.

When the need arose for someone to manage the finances of Bellingham Evangelical Free Church, Charlie Culbertson was recruited for the job, even though he had limited expertise in financial matters. For several years, Culbertson had served in Thailand with Campus Crusade for Christ. Eventually he was overseeing ministries on several campuses.

When senior pastor Gus Bess went looking for an executive pastor, it was Culbertson's heart and mind for ministry that made the difference. "The church felt they could more easily hone my financial skills than a heart for ministry," says Charlie.

Some churches take this idea a step further by requiring anyone serving on any committee to complete a cycle of training in ministry first. In my work with churches, I coach them to train people in the basics of the Christian faith and then equip them to reproduce those basics in the life of another individual. Only then will they be asked to serve in advanced forms of ministry.

In the church I attend in Bellingham, Washington, no one is allowed to serve in leadership positions of any kind without first completing a basic course in discipleship. That course includes at least one session on stewardship — and those asked to serve in leadership are asked to model faithful stewardship.

As people involve themselves in personal ministry first, they are better equipped to serve on boards and committees with a ministry mindset.

Communicate Biblical Principles of Finances

Sometimes we who have been steeped in what the Bible says about finances and ministry can forget that others have not. I have found that I cannot take for granted that even long-time attenders of the church have built their understanding on Scripture. Without solid, consistent teaching on the priority of ministry, leaders may well have other values.

Nonministry values are especially tough — and necessary —

to overcome when a ministry seems dependent on the bottom line. But it can be done. The church I attend is headed into a major building program. After seven years of existence, over a thousand people attend and ten people are on staff. To encourage people to give to the building fund, the pastor recently preached a series on giving. He had one serious reservation: during his first seven years, he had carefully cultivated a climate for outreach and discipleship; he did not want the focus to change during the building program.

He undercut the natural tendency to focus on the bottom line by emphasizing that our attitude in giving was just as important as how much we gave. The series therefore focused not merely on the giving of money but the offering up of our entire lives to God: time, talents, and treasures. All that we are, and all that we have, he reminded us, has been given to us as a trust.

Throughout the sermon series, various ministries were featured. Testimonies were given during worship. The pastor consistently shared stories about opportunities for ministry in the new building.

In short, as important as they were, the enormous financial needs of a building program were not allowed to take precedence over people and ministry.

Devise a Plan for Ministry

A finance committee is much more likely to be ministry minded if it's in a church that is ministry minded. That requires an overall plan for ministry. Here are some of the fundamental but often overlooked principles I follow in helping churches develop such a plan.

● *Define the congregation's purpose.* "More failures in the church come about because of an ambiguity of purpose than for any other reason," observes Howard Hendricks, professor at Dallas Theological Seminary in Texas.

A good mission statement answers the question, "Why do we exist as an organization?" or as I like to put it, "What on earth is the church supposed to be doing, for heaven's sake?" The mission statement of a church is the foundation upon which every ministry program is established.

• *Nurture vision.* I often travel on the Washington State ferries. Recently I was standing at the stern of one of these ships as it departed Edmonds, Washington, headed for Kingston.

A woman began to walk away when her husband asked her, "Where are you going, dear?"

"To the front of the boat," she replied. "I want to see where I'm going, not where I've been."

Actually, if you look at a ferry boat from a distance, it's hard to discern whether that vessel is coming or going, because the ship looks the same from both ends.

Some churches don't know whether they are coming or going. Others focus on where they've come from. In either case, faulty vision will impair effective ministry. Kennon Callahan, author of *Twelve Keys to an Effective Church*, observes that "Growing churches believe that their best days are ahead of them . . . declining churches believe their best days are behind them."

The vision of a church is its dream for ministry. And it is the role of leadership to keep that vision before God's people: "Where there is no vision, the people perish."

A key way to develop vision is to ask, as I did at my last church when I arrived, "What kind of church do we want to be five years from now?" When taken seriously, that question will have profound implications for administrative structures, staffing, and facilities.

• *Set congregational goals.* After setting corporate vision, set specific goals to begin to move toward realizing that vision. Webster's first definition of the word *goal* is "the terminal point of a race."

A goal is a specific plan to achieve a specific result within a specific time period. A typical church goal would be introduced by the phrase, "During the next twelve months we plan to . . ." Goals should be revised regularly in order to keep pace with a changing environment.

In any case, a goal is a statement of faith, giving concrete expression to what we believe God is leading us to accomplish.

• *Determine priorities.* Not all goals can be accomplished at once. A ministry-minded church must sort priorities, determining which goals to pursue first, second, and third: "Do we build a building first or hire a staff member?" "Do we increase our giving to missions or add an outreach locally for youth?"

One of my cardinal convictions is that staff should take priority over programs and facilities. Staff will establish programs that will minister to people, and then buildings can be built to accommodate the needs of a growing ministry.

Priorities must also be established within every area of the ministry. Should the youth ministry department invest its time and resources in major events or in small-group ministry? Should the music and worship team do a major cantata this Christmas or develop a traveling music group?

If someone left $100,000 to your church in their will, what would you do with it? Answering that is a good way to start taking seriously the need for establishing priorities. It's a way to get people to see that they don't have time and money to do everything at once.

• *Develop a plan of action.* As we prioritize our goals, we must also develop a specific action plan for achieving them. A strategic action plan will define the action steps for each goal area, the deadline for carrying them out, the person responsible for each action step, and the budget needed to carry it out.

In a church that is ministry minded, then, the financial considerations come last. Ministry planning begins with purpose, moves through dreams, goals, priorities, and plans. Only then comes consideration of the dollar. When churches follow this outline, finance committees are biased to become ministry minded.

Let Ministry Leaders Determine Needs

It's vital that the budget process begins not with how much money a church has or can expect to have but with the needs it wants to meet. I've seen at least two ways to do that: from the top down and from the bottom up.

At Hillcrest Chapel in Bellingham, the budgeting process,

described by administrative Pastor Bob Patton as "ministry driven," begins with the elders, which includes the pastoral staff. Their conviction is that the vision for ministry comes from the pastors, as God guides them. Staff members work with lay leaders to derive a plan for ministry, which results in a budget proposal to the church board.

The congregation ultimately reviews and approves the budget, but the kinks are worked out well in advance of the vote. Needless to say, this process begins well in advance of their congregational meeting. As a result of this well-orchestrated process, Hillcrest has not had serious conflict over the area of finances in the past fifteen years.

Across town at Immanuel Bible Church, the process begins with the rank and file of ministry. Marc Mullen, the church chairman, explains that people directly involved with a ministry help formulate the budget with those who oversee their ministry. For example, the leaders of junior high ministry would meet with the overall leaders of the youth ministry. An elder and a staff member are usually a part of these discussions as well. Budget figures are determined not only by needs but also by the goals and objectives of each ministry.

In addition, office staff submit their budget requests for office supplies, and the nursery coordinator requests her budget for disposable diapers — details that no pastor or finance committee is in a position to know about.

In either case, it's people involved in ministry, at one level or another, who decide what the church really needs in the coming year.

Plan for More and for Less

When a church is prepared to answer the questions, "What will we do if we have more money than expected?" and "What will we do if we have less?" it will keep mere numbers from dominating the discussion when those contingencies arise.

Bethany Bible Church in Phoenix has such a plan. Dick Stunden, the church administrator, says they always have more needs than funds available. If they project $975,000 income but receive from various ministry departments requests for $1,000,000, they will generally plug in an extra $25,000 into income as a "faith factor," trusting God for the difference. If the difference is greater, they begin restructuring the budget.

If they do have to cut back, then they let the individual ministries decide how exactly they will do that. If the youth commission, for instance, has requested $40,000 but only $30,000 becomes available, the board kicks the decision as to what to cut to the youth pastor and lay staff. They feel that each department is in a better position than the finance committee to know what they can and cannot live without. Such a procedure also makes the staff and lay leaders feel they are more in control of their ministries.

Present Financial Information to Inspire Vision

For years I received the monthly newsletter from a church I had once served as a staff member. Every month the report showed a deficit. I often wondered how they kept their doors open if they were always behind. And yet I know that during that time the staff was paid, an addition was added to the building, and the church's mortgage was later burned.

Obviously, the financial statement wasn't reflecting reality. If nothing else, a financial statement ought to do that. But if it can also inspire vision, so much the better. Then not only will the congregation and finance people know reality but they will also see clearly how finances fit into the church's goals.

One way to do this is to help the finance people figure out ways of presenting their financial information so that it inspires vision. Here are some ways I've seen congregations do that.

● *Give more exposure to people than to paper.* Lives changed demonstrate that the church is fulfilling its purpose. Testimonies remind us to focus on believers over budgets, and on ministry over money. Placing people instead of just financial reports in front of the church calls us back to our purpose — it reminds us why we're in business.

Bethany Baptist Church in Puyallup, Washington, has

recently launched a three-year financial campaign to expand its ministry. Each Sunday for the six weeks prior to the kick-off banquet, individuals gave their testimonies about how the church affected their lives. One person shared how the church had provided him and his family strength and stability in the midst of a career change and a move. A young man told how the church had stood by him while his father succumbed to cancer. And on it went.

"While our campaign goal is to expand the financial base of the church and provide facilities for ministry," says pastor Lowell Bakke, "we don't want to forget that the church revolves around people first."

● *Have an annual celebration instead of an annual meeting.* The Orchards Community Church in Lewiston, Idaho, recently had an annual business meeting that drew twice the normal crowd. The meeting was held after the Sunday morning worship service and included a fellowship dinner with tables decorated with flowers and balloons. Trays of slides depicting the ministry were interspersed with business items and testimonies of God's faithfulness. Letters from people who had moved away but were thankful for the church's ministry to them were read.

They also held a dedication service for newly elected board members, with the new members kneeling on the platform. The meeting was so meaningful for people that afterward some attenders requested membership applications.

● *Use images, not just numbers.* Campus Crusade for Christ has an entire media ministry that prepares its annual report on behalf of the staff. Through a combination of slides, video, graphics, and background music and voice, the entire ministry is featured in a thirty-minute presentation. The result is that everyone's vision is expanded as they see the worldwide scope of its ministry.

Some churches assign one or two people to take videos through the year at various church activities. Testimonials could even be recorded in advance and woven into a total ministry report.

People give to what they can see — that's why building programs tend to generate more money than less visible ministry. Our job in presenting financial information is to help people "see" the ministry that is taking place behind the budget.

One way to accomplish that is to print budget reports that show expenses and receipts in pie charts or graphs.

In addition, if a report has to be given orally, it should be short and concise as well as focused on ministry. Many churches find that the best person for this job is a lay person. The reason is that staff are usually not neutral parties in the budget; they have a vested interest in their areas of ministry as well as their compensation package. By having a lay leader address financial issues, the church takes ownership for this important area of ministry.

● *Prepare clear financial reports and budgets.* When executive pastor Charlie Culbertson took over his post at the Bellingham Evangelical Free Church, he found that the budget reports caused his eyes to glaze over trying to make sense of them. Says Culbertson, "The budget was arranged somewhat randomly, and it was full of excessive detail. So I rearranged the budget in terms of major categories, and now I report only in terms of those larger categories."

Three categories that Culbertson chose, for instance, were (1) staffing, which includes all expenses related to keeping pastors employed in the church, such as salaries, housing allowances, benefits, and business expenses; (2) facilities, which includes rent, utilities, repairs, maintenance, and office supplies; and (3) missions, which includes all programming expenses, such as youth ministry and women's ministry.

"We can now generate reports that include all the information or relatively little," says Culbertson, "depending on how much people want to see. For monthly elder meetings, though, I prepare a one- or two-page summary showing income versus expenses and the balance in church accounts. The elders don't need to deal with the vast volume of details regularly. And for a quick update to the congregation, I'll use pie charts."

Certainly, finance committees will have to spend the bulk of their time crunching numbers — they're the committee that is given this arduous task. But there is no reason why the nature of their task has to determine how they view their task. They can be structured so that instead of numbers and pledge cards, the Lord and his vision for the church inspire their work.

Preaching about money is one of the most spiritual things I do.

— *Wayne Pohl*

CHAPTER THREE

The Spiritual Side of Mammon

I was sitting with a young couple interested in church membership. As I had planned, part of the conversation hinged on money. I explained our church's understanding of generosity and tithing, highlighting several Scriptures and sharing what a difference these principles had made in our church's life. I finished with, "I want you to know we're a tithing congregation. We welcome you to become a part of our church, but if tithing bothers you, you may be more comfortable elsewhere."

The husband replied, "Pastor, we attend church weekly, and

we've always donated five dollars a week. My parents always gave five dollars a week. I really don't know how we could do what you're describing." He was in shock.

Nevertheless, they eventually joined our church, and by the time they moved away, they were contributing 13 percent of their income.

Preaching what Scripture says about money is volatile, revolutionary, risky business. "Money makes the world go round." It keeps dinner on the table and the wolf from the door. Money means comfort, power, security, status, opportunity, freedom, pleasure, choice. That is why Christ makes radical claims on our checkbooks. No other issue so clearly, objectively addresses the clash between this world's values and Christian values: "You cannot serve God and Mammon."

Preaching about money is thus one of the most spiritual things I do. It is one of the most practical ways I can help people grow in their faith. It is also a subject full of danger if not presented well. Here are some things I keep in mind as I touch on this vital topic.

Avoiding Misunderstandings

I enjoy preaching about money, though I admit, it is the tense joy a lion tamer feels in a cage full of growling man-eaters. Money makes people tense and talking about it can create a lot of misunderstandings, some of which can be hazardous for the health of a congregation.

To avoid such misperceptions, I follow these guidelines.

• *Warn visitors.* A young couple attended a friend's church one Sunday. They liked the service so much they came back the next week. That week, my friend, a pastor, happened to be giving his annual sermon on tithing. When he visited them the next day, one of the first things they brought up was their concern about the church's emphasis on money.

If regular attenders are skittish about the subject of money, how much more are newcomers. I don't want them to think, *All they want is my money.*

So I warn visitors before I begin talking about money. In fact, they are the only people I ever apologize to when talking about money. I tell them, "You didn't come here today to hear about our budget. We hope that you'll understand that it needs to be talked about sometimes, and this is our time. I can assure you, we don't talk about it for the rest of the year."

• *Base the sermon in Scripture.* I do this because I don't want to give anyone the impression that I'm self-serving when I preach about money. At all costs, I want to avoid the appearance that I'm seeking my own glory or the church's glory. I not only preach from Scripture, I periodically mention that I am preaching on the topic because Scripture calls me to. I have no choice.

• *Preach tithing seldom.* Even generous givers may feel I'm coming on too strong or that we talk about it too much, making money too high a priority. Many people gladly receive preaching on finances but rightfully resist being nagged about it. Overdoing it is counterproductive: it turns people off and makes it more difficult in the future to talk about finances.

Consequently, we limit preaching on finances to two weeks out of the year. I believe that if we do our job well during this emphasis, people will respond positively and will generously fulfill their financial responsibilities to God for the rest of the year.

Our stewardship month — highlighting God's ownership of our time, talents, and treasures — is held every November, a month when few are traveling or otherwise distracted. I talk about our finances for two of the four stewardship Sundays (by the way, outside of Christmas and Easter, these two Sundays have occasionally been our best attended Sundays in the year).

I promise the congregation, "If you do your part this week, and if you follow through, you won't hear a sermon specifically about money for another year." In other messages during the year, I will, from time to time, refer to finances if the text touches on it. But I won't preach a full sermon on it except in November.

• *Don't promise anything God doesn't.* One woman in our church was in poverty. We helped her with food, clothing, and housing for quite some time. Eventually she left our church for another. A year later she phoned me and asked, "Can I borrow

$1,000 from you personally?"

"That's an interesting request," I replied.

"Reverend Pohl, this will help me so much. My pastor said last week that if we bring $1,000 to the church, within a month $2,000 would be returned to us. I'll pay you back when that money comes."

I had a problem with that. I do believe what Malachi says, that God will return to tithers even more than they gave, that we can't outgive God. But I don't teach what this other church did, and I'm careful not to even suggest it. In fact, during stewardship month, during which our members tell stories about how the Lord has worked through their giving, I screen stories beforehand for such ideas. I don't want anyone disillusioned with God, who returns to us in times and ways we can't predict, because I have overstated his promises.

• *Don't whine.* Under financial pressure, we can fall into a negative attitude. In the you're-a-dirty-rat approach, we complain that people aren't doing enough. We tell how we are suffering because of the church's financial straits, trying to motivate giving from sympathy or guilt, directly or indirectly fixing blame.

Whining is counterproductive. Newer members don't feel enough ownership of the church or affection for the pastor to sacrifice. Often whining scares them away.

It doesn't motivate long-time members either, at least for the long term. It merely prods the old faithfuls to do more because they dislike seeing the pastor cry in public. It can also breed resentment, so that even if people's giving meets the need, the new wine of church life turns sour.

The only way to undercut whining is to preach a positive stewardship: God has given us much; we grow in our relationship to him as we give to him; giving does great things for the kingdom and for us.

• *Raise people first.* I lead our church by the philosophy that you don't grow dollars, you grow people. When you cultivate people, dollars will come. Because discipling Christians is our real objective, I never preach about money alone — what giving will do for this project or that — but always in terms of our relationship to God, in terms of our stewardship of time, talents, and treasures. The more I preach about how giving relates to a person's love relationship with God, the more their lifestyle and perspective will change.

Growing people is not an ulterior motive for extracting money. One of the kindest things I can do for people is to teach them God's financial principles. Their spiritual growth depends on it.

Helping People Become Generous

One pastor in Illinois was speaking with a parishioner about tithing. The parishioner, who said he believed in tithing and in the need to be generous beyond the tenth, said, "Pastor, instead of tithing to our church I contribute to the needy. In fact, I am giving very generously."

"Do me a favor," his pastor said. "Pull out your check registers this week and total your charitable giving for the year. I believe your motives, but I know human nature. I would be willing to bet you're not giving as much as you think. Compare your giving with your gross income and see if you are truly 'tithing' to the needy."

The parishioner became angry. He stayed up late into the night poring over his records, determined to prove his pastor wrong. Several days later, he phoned his pastor: "I can't believe it. You're right. I haven't been close to giving a tenth of my income."

Many who suppose they are generous really aren't because they haven't retooled their budget. Stellar ideals have to make their way into the checkbook. Here are some of the ways I encourage that.

● *Discuss giving only in the context of stewardship.* The theme of stewardship keeps the subject of giving in the proper perspective. People see giving as it relates to God rather than merely to the church or me, as Paul says in 2 Corinthians 8:5, "They gave themselves first to the Lord and then to us." When people know why God gave them their money and possessions, what God has called our church to do, and why God has placed them in our congregation, they are highly motivated givers rather than reluctant payers of dues.

During our Loyalty Month (stewardship month), we emphasize God's ownership, his rightful claim on our time, talents, and treasure. Money is only part of the picture. We talk specifically about how members can employ their spiritual gifts. We encourage people to carve time in their schedules for Christian growth and ministry. I have found that once Christians wholeheartedly dedicate their lives to God, financial giving becomes a natural response to his love.

During the rest of the year, even when I'm preaching on texts that address the subject of money directly, I still make stewardship of *all* we have the backdrop of the message. When I preach on the story of Jesus watching the widow give her last mite, for example, I approach that passage in terms of what it means to live a life where you give everything to God. Secondarily I would apply that to finances. My goal is to develop a congregation with a *lifestyle* of sacrifice, dedication, and stewardship.

• *Show the benefits.* I present giving as a privilege, as an opportunity. I show how it benefits others, glorifies God, and benefits ourselves. Even when talking about stewardship as a responsibility, I highlight the beautiful righteousness of that duty, that stewardship isn't a burden but rather a high calling from a God who actually trusts his people. It *is* more blessed to give than to receive. When people give, they aren't losing, they're gaining in multiplied ways.

More specifically, by presenting next year's budget during Loyalty Month, I show the exciting things that their donations will enable in our church. We tell them about goals for additional staff, building plans, new programs and ministries, and people being helped. Members enjoy seeing the difference giving makes. I tell people, "Your giving makes the angels sing. Your giving is bringing others to Christ, and heaven is rejoicing."

• *Emphasize percentages.* People need concrete giving goals and objective ways of determining whether they've reached them. So I challenge people to donate specific amounts, and I word my challenge so that it makes an impact: I emphasize *percentage* giving.

We don't emphasize dollar giving because I don't want to

discourage low-wage earners who are nevertheless generous. The teenager who earns $4.50 an hour mowing the funeral home lawn and contributes 15 percent to the church should take as much pride in his sacrifice as the millionaire who donates 15 percent. If I mention the man who donates $30,000 to the building fund but ignore the woman on social security who gives 13 percent (maybe $33 a week) of her income, I have discouraged sacrificial giving among the majority in my congregation.

For example, when one of our middle-class families pledged $50,000 to the three-year building, we lauded not the amount but that this would be 23 ½ percent of their income.

When discussing percentage giving, I highlight two principles for people.

1. Tithing is a guideline. I preach tithing through Scripture first. I turn to 2 Corinthians to show how the New Testament encourages percentage giving and regular giving; then we observe in the Old Testament how the tenth was a significant percentage.

But I'm not legalistic. People aren't going to go to hell because they donate 8 percent instead of 10. Teaching on tithing draws flak, but I'm not willing to settle for the lowest common denominator. In fact, I say generosity really begins after the tithe.

I supplement my preaching about tithing by inviting people to tell in worship about their own experiences with tithing. I'm not looking for rags-to-riches miracle stories. I want them instead to emphasize the spiritual effects of their giving.

An engineer, a long-time tither, lost his job when his employer went out of business. He stood before the congregation and described how their income and "standard of living" had fallen two-thirds.

Although they were living on his wife's income alone, they were determined to continue tithing. "God has done great things in our lives during this time. We have seen his provision in ways we didn't when we had all we needed and wanted. If you put God to the test, he will bless you. He keeps his promises."

2. Experiment and keep growing. I encourage people to start where their faith is and grow from there. Some new converts enter

the church drowning in debt and obligations. For them, tithing is either impossible or unthinkable. So I challenge them to stretch to give whatever percentage they can. And as their lives get ordered by God and their faith in him increases, I encourage them to stretch their giving.

The Trust Factor

The hidden ingredient in my preaching is the most important in helping people give generously: trust. If people trust me, if they trust our leaders and policies and process, if they trust our Lord, they will give year after year. Suggestions for giving and programs to raise money have their place, but they are meaningless without trust.

My most important concern, then, is building trust. Two elements lay the foundation of trust in my preaching.

1. A long-term ministry. It's unrealistic to expect to gain complete trust in one year of ministry. We know our hearts, but others don't. It takes time for people to know us. It takes time for a pastor to prove himself.

Someone has said, "A pastor must serve a congregation for three years before the people know him, another two years before they love him, and another two before they trust him." After serving seventeen years at this church, people know my every wart. They know my positives and my negatives. Even if they don't agree with me, they know my motives; they know I would sacrifice anything for this church. And they know my pattern of financial giving.

A good track record speaks volumes. People need not only to know a pastor's heart but also to know he can deliver sound, skilled, and responsible leadership. A pastor has to prove himself equal to challenges. Again, that takes time.

2. Total disclosure. When a pastor or church curtains information, people logically wonder why. Secrecy breeds curiosity, suspicion, and gossip faster than darkness brings out cockroaches. Total disclosure opens the windows to the sunlight of trust.

We have no hidden agendas. At our annual meeting, we distribute financial reports as complete as any corporation provides its shareholders. Our board of directors meets every month, and the meeting is open for anyone in the congregation to observe.

If things go wrong, we never stonewall. In our recent building program we raised funds by selling properties. One buyer offered $525,000 for 14.6 acres, a sum of money we were planning on heavily. Then the Environmental Protection Agency spotted a red-shouldered hawk on the property. They declared it a wetland, and the buyer flew away.

Whenever something goes wrong, even if they have done everything right, leaders take some heat. Nevertheless we immediately called a meeting of the church and briefed the people. "In the long run we will be all right," I told them. "We'll eventually get the money out of this property, but in the short run we are going to have to scramble." Because of this difficulty, we did lose momentum, but we didn't lose trust or donations.

In addition to these two elements, one practice builds trust as I preach: *Letting people see me as a giver who is still growing.*

People trust a leader whose lifestyle is true to his words. But my example must be given with great care; it cannot be a sanctimonious display. I attended a meeting once when the pastor at the pulpit pulled out his checkbook and wrote out his check from the pulpit. Nothing wrong with that necessarily, but his manner did not motivate me to give. I felt manipulated.

Nevertheless I do divulge my giving, but in a way that shows I'm still in process, even struggling. For example, in our recent building-fund drive, I told the people that I had initially committed a significant percentage above our tithe, to be given over several years.

Then I said, "Giving this much scared me. But when I told my wife what I thought we should pledge, she looked at me across the table and said, 'That's not enough.'

"I was ready to strangle her. We've got two kids at Michigan State University as well as the bills everyone else has. But in the end, she convinced me to pledge another $1,400 in all. She has the gift of giving. I certainly don't."

In this case, I was also able to show the congregation how God had dealt with my anxiety, within a month no less. Groaning under sky-high auto insurance rates and owning two cars driven also by a 23-year-old and a 17-year-old, I called around to price various insurance agencies. I discovered a company that only insures teachers and their families. Since my wife is a teacher I investigated: because teachers are conservative and cautious people, legendary for safe driving, that company quoted us an annual fee $1,400 less than we were paying.

"This doesn't always happen," I reminded the people. "We don't know how God will work when we give in faith and what will happen to our 'standard of living,' but we do know that somehow God will meet our needs. Somehow we will see the hand of God in our finances."

Many people regard their wallets as no one else's business. When a pastor preaches on stewardship, they feel he's meddling. But I'm not intimidated. I march boldly and unapologetically into the lion's cage, knowing that I'm helping people be all that God wants: generous, unselfish, fully committed disciples of Jesus Christ.

Many pastors don't like to think of themselves as fundraisers, but the function seems to go with the position. And whether we like it or not, the better we fulfill that part of our job, the more effective our ministries.

— Gary Fenton

CHAPTER FOUR

The Moneywise Pastor

There is an old story about a young seminary graduate who came to a rural congregation as their first seminary-trained pastor. The people were proud of his vocabulary, the evidences of culture and education, and his sophistication.

Several weeks after his arrival, he announced that on the following Sunday he would speak on "The Fiduciary Stewardship of the Royal Priesthood." The congregation eagerly anticipated this learned young man's sermon.

When the minister completed the sermon, one of the members said, "Pastor, I don't know exactly what it was you preached about, but it sounded like what our former pastor used to say when he was trying to lift an offering."

Regardless of how we say it, we are fund raisers in the eyes of many people. Many pastors don't like to think of themselves that way, but the function seems to go with the position. And whether we like it or not, the better we fulfill that part of our job, the more effective our ministries.

Why Become Involved

I have heard a few pastors say that they don't become involved in the financial procedures of the church — although I have heard very few say this in the presence of their church members! As much as I sometimes rebel against the idea, I've come up with several reasons I take an active role in the financial procedures of the church.

● *The pastor is a part of the church family.* For a member to be ignorant of how the church is actually using its funds would amount to poor stewardship. If church members are expected to be at least somewhat informed and interested in church finances, I'm no exception.

● *The pastor is a church leader.* The precise role of the pastor as leader varies from church to church, but for me to avoid all involvement in church finances would be to abdicate leadership. It takes money to build buildings, pay salaries, supply paper clips, and offer curriculum materials. I've never seen a church that can do without such things. Therefore I don't think I can claim to lead a church if I don't, at some level, concern myself with how it's going to pay for paper clips.

And as a leader I don't want to communicate a cavalier attitude about money. An older and wiser minister, speaking to our staff, told us that by refusing to become involved in money issues, we tell our people that money is not important.

Some pastors say they want to reserve their energies for the more "spiritual" concerns and leave money matters to others. I find it difficult, however, to separate money from spiritual issues. Jesus addressed the subject of money often, and his interest in the subject didn't make his ministry less spiritual.

● *Only the pastor sees the big picture.* In one church I served, a staff member suggested to me that our annual stewardship appeal actually discouraged new members from giving. At the time, our church was having difficulty assimilating new members into the life of the church. Although the motto and budget letter had not consciously excluded new members, it could have been interpreted that way.

Since the overall finances were not in this staff person's responsibility, he had hesitated to speak to the finance committee. Even if he had, the finance committee, because it is not directly concerned with membership, may not have taken his objection seriously. After I discussed the matter with the committee, they agreed to make some necessary changes.

As pastor, I was the only person in the church who was aware and concerned about both issues (new members and finances) and had the clout to make sure both were taken seriously.

Five Ways to Raise Funds

To be involved with finances, though, doesn't mean we have to master the intricacies of spreadsheets. I've found I can be involved in five less tangible but perhaps more crucial ways.

1. Stewardship preacher. We live in a materialistic society, and often the first line of spiritual skirmish in believers is at the point of spending. Naturally, stewardship is more than asking for money, but it certainly includes money. As I mentioned, Jesus touched on money often in his preaching. I am wise to do no less. And if I do it well, it will raise money for the church.

And that means I've got to get specific from time to time.

"Why don't you use the word *money* when preaching about stewardship?" a member once asked me. "You speak of resources, talents, possessions, tithing, and sacrificial giving, but you appear to be afraid of the word *money*." After verbally treading water for several minutes, I had to admit he was right. I avoided the word *money* as if it were obscene.

When preaching on stewardship now, I try to use the M-word as well as *talents, time,* and the other "good" words. Not only is it more effective, it is also more honest. Sometimes when we ask people to give money, we need to make ourselves clear that this is what we are asking for. I am still not perfectly comfortable with it, but that's *my* problem. I don't have to project that upon the whole church.

2. *Accidental fund raiser.* Most people want to give to a variety of causes. And they often become aware of a cause, and thus contribute to it, because they've heard about it first in a sermon or class I've given. When, as a sermon illustration, I mention the work of the local food closet or a Baptist missionary, people will sometimes approach me afterwards asking how they can donate to the person or organization I've mentioned.

Also, I sometimes inadvertently challenge people to give when I address deeper issues in their lives. Once after I preached a message on compassion for the outcast, a man made a commitment to give a large amount to the benevolence ministry of our church. My message made no reference to money. I was seeking to address the attitude of superiority most upwardly mobile people have when they associate with the poor. This wealthy man heard his greed and selfishness challenged.

3. *A trusted trustee.* To many members, the pastor is the one person they can talk to without feeling manipulated. The pastor is wise to preserve this trust, especially when it comes to financial matters.

A wealthy and generous layman told me in any given week he received five to eight requests for charitable contributions. He had the same pastor for over twenty years and had developed a healthy respect for him. He said that when his pastor indicated a need in the church or the community, he was more than willing to give, because his pastor had never, to his knowledge, abused the gift or tried to manipulate him for selfish purposes.

4. *Herald of the vision.* The pastor may not be the only one who reminds the congregation of the church's goals, but he or she is usually the best trained to put the vision into words and images that

a broad spectrum of the congregation can appreciate. People give to causes that flow out of the vision. I don't articulate a vision for the sole purpose of raising money, but if I cast vision well, I see money raised.

5. *The conscience of the church.* The pastor, among others, must insist on integrity in financial matters. The pastor publicly and privately must be aware of how money is raised, given, counted, and spent, and how all this is reported.

In some cases, the issues are not so subtle. In one large church, the budget promotion committee planned a stewardship campaign that used a slogan and creative publicity methods. Unfortunately, they appealed to guilt and greed. The pastor intervened and asked the committee to redesign their emphasis. Although two leaders at first felt the pastor was trying to usurp their authority, they finally saw the pastor's point.

In some instances, though, the lack of integrity is subtle. In one church, the new pastor heard several people complain about the complexity of the monthly financial statement. When he asked the treasurer and the chairman of the board of deacons, they explained to him how to interpret the statement. After a couple of hours of decoding, the pastor determined that the church was in great financial condition. Still, it wasn't right, he thought, that the financial statement was too difficult to understand without detailed explanations.

As the pastor researched the problem, he discovered that the previous pastor and treasurer had designed the financial statement to keep the people from asking questions about expenditures. The report had been intentionally designed to intimidate the congregation into silence! Consequently, the questions about finances usually centered on the form of reporting, and there never seemed to be enough time to discuss exactly how money was being used.

The pastor quickly recognized this as a lack of integrity in reporting finances, and he eventually led the treasurer to present more clearly the information.

What to Say in a Finance Committee Meeting

In most churches the pastor is an ex-officio member of all the committees of the church, including the finance committee. As such, the pastor is permitted to discuss issues but not vote on them. How and where to become involved in the discussion of financial matters is a crucial issue for the pastor. I have found the following guidelines helpful.

● *Speak to clarify.* The pastor is often the only person who represents continuity in a committee. Church committees are in constant transition, and the people in them, or many of them at least, may be asked to discuss issues of which they have little knowledge. If an embryo of confusion exists in financial matters, I find it helps everyone if I speak up.

Recently in a finance committee meeting, a staff member realized that several new members did not understand the purpose of a proposed change in our financial policy. The change, in fact, was insignificant, more a housekeeping item than a major policy shift, but the new members couldn't have known that.

The staff member noticed one of the new members start to ask a question but then withdraw, mumbling that his question was not worthy of the time required to discuss it. The staff member at this point asked to speak to clarify what exactly was going on. Soon the hesitant new members were "on board" and happily supported the change.

● *Speak when you are the only source of information.* The pastor sometimes has privileged information that the committee needs if it's going to make an intelligent decision.

In one church I served, the finance committee was concerned over the church's heating bills. Our church purchased propane from a local businessman, who was not a member of the church. It was moved by a committee member immediately to begin a bidding process with other companies.

I happened to know that at the end of each year, we received a check for our building fund from this businessman. Although the check equaled our annual billing to his company, he insisted on anonymity.

Without giving all the details, I assured the committee, "Changing companies at this time would prove quite expensive to the church. For one reason, this man's company has been quite generous to our church for several years, which more than compensates for the relatively high heating bills."

The matter was then dropped.

● *Speak redemptively regarding controversial issues.* Financial issues are great arenas for controversy. Sometimes individuals or groups become polarized and often question the motives of those who differ with them. But often the pastor can bring unity to the group.

One pastor, after hearing members debate a controversial program, tried to interpret positively each view he had heard.

On the one hand, there were some who were opposed to the proposed bond program to finance the program. These people seemed to be less opposed to the program than to the method. This was a valid concern, he concluded.

The pastor also mentioned those who had reservations regarding the timing of the program. These people thought a large program like the one proposed needed more time to develop. These folks, the pastor explained, did not want to block the church's vision, they simply wanted to ensure the program's success.

The pastor also discussed the views of those who supported the program. His purpose was to show that each position had merit and that to support one did not mean you had to question the integrity of the other positions or their proponents.

The pastor then explained why he supported the bond program, but he made it clear that it was not a vote between good and evil but a vote between three options, which were all morally good.

The layman who told me this story said that although the pastor's preference of proceeding with the bond program had probably been a minority position at the start of the meeting, the committee voted to support the pastor's position and did so with a sense of unity.

● *Affirm major decisions.* After a committee has approved a large expenditure or is facing a deficit, it's important to reassure them of the decision they've made.

Churches usually elect people to finance committees who will protect the church's investments: bankers, accountants, and financial managers. The problem is such people have been trained to minimize loss rather than produce great gain. They are the kinds of people who feel personally responsible for the church's finances. So they tend to see more risk and problems than exist.

I feel one of my roles is to keep reminding the committee of the things that are going well and of the signs that the future is hopeful. This doesn't mean that I understate the gravity of any situation. I've just discovered a church's financial problems are usually not as grave as they first appear. They may not be solvable in one committee meeting, but over the long run, they usually can be worked out.

Sometimes we help a committee think about their difficult work in hopeful terms. The church in which I presently serve went through a major financial crisis prior to my coming. Due to an intense conflict, several of the church's long-time "financial heavy hitters" had left the church. During the interim, the financial leadership had to prepare a budget.

Everyone knew that the church would have to reduce the budget from the previous year, but people were divided over how to go about the cuts. Some wanted immediate and drastic reductions, others less drastic. The committee prepared a budget that tried to please both sides, but in the end everyone on the committee felt as if the cuts they had made were pretty brutal.

The interim pastor at this point stepped in and spoke to the committee: "I know how difficult it can be to be good stewards in a time like this. I also know we have to make some necessary reductions, and that is going to create some pain among the members. But let's remember that the work you've done here is the first step in getting us in shape for the future.

"Don't think of yourselves as butchers, hacking away at excess fat. Think of yourselves as aerobic instructors; you're dealing with fat by exercise and good diet. That's going to be painful, but in the end it will be worth it. The whole church will be more healthy."

Instead of the reduced budget being a brutal and defeating experience, it became a watershed budget that made it possible for the church to be a good steward to this day.

Delegating Financial Matters

The pastor, in order to be effective, must delegate some fiscal responsibilities. Each community and each church has different expectations regarding the role of the pastor. A careful exegesis of the local culture of the community will help the pastor learn to deal with these expectations and keep the church directed toward its specific mission.

● *Clarify what is delegated.* Each church has unique traditions, so the job titles and descriptions of committees and boards will not necessarily reflect accurately what each does. When dealing with money issues, it is imperative that everyone know what is being delegated and to whom.

In one large church, a new pastor arrived just prior to the preparation of the budget. He assumed that the budget preparation committee would promote the budget — at least that's what the committee job description indicated. But by tradition, the staff and church council actually promoted the budget. There was mass confusion in his first year and a shortfall in pledges. As a result, it took several years for the church to recover.

That pastor now writes an annual expectation letter to the finance committee chairperson. He tells the chairperson precisely what he can expect from the pastor and the staff, and he then lists what he expects of the chairperson. In his letter, he invites the chairperson to redefine or change the expectations.

● *Determine how much you should know about individual contributions.* Before deciding how much I should know about people's giving, I ask myself two key questions.

1. What is the tradition of the church? A pastor friend recently interviewed with a church's search committee. He said he received more questions regarding how he handled financial contributions than how he preached or practiced spiritual disciplines.

Specifically, they said they did not want their pastor to know the amounts of people's giving. They felt their previous pastor spent inordinate time with the people who lived in the "high-tithe district." More than likely, their new pastor will have limited access to members' giving patterns, at least for a few years while these wounds heal.

Other churches expect the pastor to know the giving records of the members. They feel that as shepherd of the flock, he needs this information in order to hold the membership accountable for their stewardship. These churches often have a tradition of trust and confidence in their pastors.

If a pastor is still uncomfortable knowing about members' giving, he will have to explain carefully why he wants to remain ignorant of such things. Otherwise, the members may interpret his lack of interest as an indication that stewardship is not important to him.

2. Can I handle this information with integrity? Will my knowing help the members and the church, or will it just get in the way of my ministry?

I have found that I'm a better pastor if I don't know the giving levels of individual members. I become angry with people who I believe are not giving enough, and my anger only increases when I feel my own family is making great sacrifices compared with them. Neither does reviewing records anonymously, without knowing the individual whose giving I'm examining, increase my effectiveness.

On the other hand, I don't hesitate to ask members about their giving when they are nominated to serve in leadership positions. Since our congregation has a strong history of tithing, I ask our prospective deacons if their giving level is consistent with the church's view of tithing and with our emphasis on sacrificial giving. If they are going to help lead the church, they have to live by our priorities.

Many churches ask the financial secretary or treasurer to review the giving records of all potential leaders prior to their election. If their giving level is not acceptable, they tell the nominating committee so. The church I serve does this for members nominated to committees that handle large sums of money.

Then again, one of the most effective pastors I know reviews annually the giving records of each of his members. He does this, he says, not for the financial good of the church but for the good of the individual member.

If a member's contributions have dropped drastically in one year, it prompts him to ask the member if the family is having a financial crisis. He has discovered some members with intense needs this way. I have known people who were members of this church, and each of them speaks positively of this practice. Apparently he did not start this practice, though, until he served this congregation several years.

Always a Shepherd

A pastor may have financial responsibilities in the church, but in the end, we're still pastors.

One recent Sunday evening, I began the sermon by asking everyone to take the largest denomination bill out of their wallet or purse. If they had nothing larger then a five, I told them to take a check out of their checkbook. I did this on my seventh-month anniversary as pastor.

The congregation looked at me as if I were joking. I told them I was serious, and I really hoped they would do as I suggested. To those who had taken out a check, I asked them to find a pen and a hymnal, or something else with a hard surface. Some nervous laughter moved through the sanctuary, but most people did what I suggested.

I took a fifty-dollar bill out of my wallet. I then paused for about a minute and looked across the congregation and commented on the tension in the room. It felt as if "the honeymoon" was over. Even those to whom I felt closest looked at me as if I had lost my mind.

After the pause, I said, "Okay, you can put away your money and checks." We all felt the tension ease.

"We're a lot more relaxed now, aren't we?" Everyone

laughed. "You think *you* were nervous; my palms are sweaty!" I continued. "We were nervous, of course, because we thought we were going to have to part with something that is precious to us. And that's uncomfortable.

"In my tenure as pastor, sometimes I or the finance committee will ask you to part with things that are valuable to you, like your money. I never want to manipulate you, but even the gentlest discussion of money can make us all feel uncomfortable. I want you to know I understand that; I feel it myself. I also want you to know that Christ can help us deal with this discomfort."

In the end, my most important financial role with my people is that of pastor. I not only help people to give to the work of the church, I also help them identify their fears and concerns, especially about money, and place such anxieties into the hands of a compassionate God.

Part Two
Raising and Monitoring Money

Money flows to the right causes.

— Wayne Pohl

CHAPTER FIVE

Developing Generous Givers

Last year, for the first time in the almost two decades that I have been pastor of St. Paul's, we had to make a 17 percent across-the-board, mid-year cut in the budget, primarily because of economic recession in the Detroit area.

But there were other reasons. Raising money is more difficult today than at any time in my twenty-five years of ministry. There are so many more toys to buy and pleasures to pursue. People want the newest technology in their homes. The percentage of our members who frequent Florida or Arizona every winter or a cabin in northern Michigan every summer weekend has increased. Such enticements divert dollars.

And there is a new mindset. Whereas our parents and grand-parents believed in saving money for security, accumulating as large an inheritance as possible for their children, today, in such uncertain times, people wonder how much time they have left. Many choose to live for the moment. One bumper sticker says, "I'm spending my child's inheritance."

Sometimes I feel like a farmer who watches better crops grow-ing in the fields but who also fights more vicious infestations of worms, crows, weeds, and blight. Raising congregational giving — so that ministry can expand, needs can be met, and people will be drawn to Christ — is becoming an ever greater challenge.

Here is how I respond.

Rivet Attention on the Great Commission

Seeds take root and grow best in rich, black topsoil. The rich-est topsoil for growing dollars for ministry is a vision for the Great Commission. If I have cast the vision clearly, if our hearts are beat-ing for the lost, finances will follow. Money flows to the right causes. Great Commission enthusiasm, in fact, provides a growth environment for every area of the church, but especially in people's financial stewardship.

Several years ago, as happens to most churches at one time or another, this congregation got comfortable. When leadership pro-posed a new and larger sanctuary, we heard objections: "We're already the largest congregation of any denomination in the south suburbs of Detroit. We already have 1,000 people attending wor-ship weekly. We've got money to hire staff and run effective pro-grams. Why do we need more people?"

When I heard such comments, I said to myself, *Pohl, you haven't focused their attention on the mission. They don't have the vision.* Good stewardship is built on a clear understanding of the church's purpose: we exist to reach the lost. That dream elicits dollars.

People ask, "Will you ever be satisfied?"

"No," I reply. "We won't be satisfied until we've reached the

52,500 unchurched people within a six-mile radius of our church. Until then, we will keep growing, expanding staff and facilities, and multiplying programs. Of necessity, this is a growing church."

Without that challenge, a church eventually relaxes, as do financial commitments. I tell people if they are rankled by a challenge, by pressure to expand ministry, there are comfortable churches to attend. If they want to be a part of something special, something with a great purpose, something exciting, then a price must be paid. Significance has a cost.

Detonate Myths

Myths about church finances abound. They are like boll weevils boring into cotton balls. I have found that I need to spray pesticides on the following myths of lay people.

● *No matter what I give, God will provide.* After one stewardship sermon, which outlined cutbacks necessary to accommodate the budget, one of the wealthier older members of our congregation greeted me warmly at the door, grabbed my arm, and said, "Pastor, God will send someone to meet our need." I had hoped she would be the one, but that never happened.

I've found the best response to those who have swallowed this myth is "Yes, the Lord will provide — through you and me and everyone in this church. If you believe what you're saying, I want you to trust the Lord to provide for *you* personally as you give sacrificially to this ministry. The Lord wants to perform a miracle not only in the church's finances but in every individual's finances."

We work to overcome this myth in membership classes. "It is a mystery," I often say, "but God has limited himself to accomplishing his work, building his church and reaching the lost through us. In this church, we're not going to beat you over the head about finances, but please know that we need you to support this church financially. Everyone does his or her part. Some churches may run on air, but we need chairs and food and utilities."

● *Normal expenses do not apply to the church.* Many people act as if the church is in a different dimension. The expenses they deal with daily — utilities, food, and a roof overhead — don't, in their minds, apply to the church or its workers. *No company would shut off a church's gas, electricity, phone, or water,* they may unthinkingly conclude. *No one would haul a church into court. The church staff gladly serves the Lord, with little concern about their wages.*

In my annual money sermon I give people a dose of reality by reading our annual expenses: "We paid over $30,000 to Michigan Consolidated Gas Company last year. We paid over $1,000 a month to Michigan Bell and AT&T. These companies have a habit of wanting to be paid. We are not of the world, but we are in the world."

One time after I made this speech, a member admitted, "Pastor, I never would have thought our church had to pay so much in phone bills. My phone bill is thirty dollars a month." I explained that we have sixteen staff people and nine lines running into the building. His eyes were opened, and soon after he increased his pledge significantly.

● *No matter what happens, everything will somehow work out for good.* Church money shortages don't bother some members. In their minds, that's the way it's supposed to be in church. Financial shortages work for good: The pastor will be more spiritual if he doesn't know one day from the next where his salary will come from or how the church mortgage will be paid. The less secure we are financially, the more members will need to trust.

I teach that while God works for good even in poverty, he doesn't oppose financial strength in his church. God doesn't want pastors pleading every week for money to pay the bills. He doesn't want the pastor's family resenting the ministry because they struggle financially. He doesn't want his church to have the reputation in the community of being a slow pay, or worse, a no pay. God doesn't want churches so weighted down with financial problems that they can't think of expanding their vision and ministry.

The stronger a church is financially, the more good it can do for God in the world, the better its reputation will be with outsiders, and the more it can help the needy. The highest good is to accomplish much for Christ.

Using the Pulpit Effectively

Preaching is the greatest tool I have to encourage people toward higher giving. By using it well, I can help people become better stewards. Here are a few guidelines I follow when preaching about money.

● *Talk about money.* I currently sit on a denominational council that deals with stewardship matters. I repeatedly hear pastors proudly say, "I never talk about money from the pulpit." It is no coincidence that many of the churches they lead are financially weak.

Clearly some pastors are hesitant, at best, to talk about money from the pulpit. Stewardship, yes. Sacrifice, yes. But money? That seems too mundane and personal.

I have never thought of it that way. People need leadership, instruction, and discipleship in every dimension of the Christian life: doctrine, marriage, child raising, thought life, speech, work. Finances are no different. I give people the whole counsel of God, especially on a subject so critical that Jesus said, "You cannot serve God and money."

In addition, if a pastor never talks about money, members won't think giving is important. Jesus thought it important enough to talk about often, so it's certainly appropriate for me to do likewise.

● *Don't talk about money more than twice a year.* I limit myself to two money sermons a year, both during stewardship month. If I preach money more than that, I've noticed diminishing returns as some people get defensive, resistant.

When I do address it, I say, "If you do your job during pledge week, you will never hear another sermon during the year on money." In my experience, people give more as a result. Knowing that they will not be hounded for money every week, they listen better when I do talk about it. They appreciate my approach: besides Christmas and Easter, the highest attended Sundays of the year often are the two Sundays I talk about money.

● *Preach as if Christians want to give.* Analysts of church culture commonly say, "Unchurched people tell us that one of the biggest reasons they avoid church is 'All they talk about is money.' " Hearing that, it doesn't take long for a pastor to conclude that Christians themselves, even committed members of a church, would rather not hear about money, don't want to be challenged to give, nor want to know about the church's needs.

While that may be true for some, my experience is that followers of Christ want to give. With the Spirit of God in their hearts, they have a predisposition to become increasingly unselfish, generous, and filled with agape love. The church is their eternal family. If we present the needs properly, believers appreciate the opportunity to give for the Lord.

One evening fifteen years ago, a young management executive in our congregation shared with me, "One of my life goals is to be the leading giver in our congregation." At the time, he owned an average home and was on a bottom rung in a multinational corporation. Nevertheless he gave enthusiastically what he could.

Bob advanced quickly in the management positions of his corporation, and he now heads a major division. About a year ago, I told him, "Bob, thank God for your commitment, and thank God for his blessings to you and this church. This past year your dream was realized. You have become the leading contributor to this congregation."

His motives were not selfish; our congregation does not publish what people give. His ambition was no different than the person who says, "I want to be the finest Sunday school teacher in our church." He simply wanted to be a giver.

● *Mention specific needs from the pulpit.* Some feel that talking about specific projects and needs from the pulpit diminishes the motive of giving purely out of love for the Lord. I look at the epistles, however, and I see Paul collecting money for the needy in Jerusalem. That doesn't mean he doesn't want the bottom-line motive for people's giving to be their love for the Lord; he is calling on them to fulfill their responsibility, to have compassion. And you can't show compassion to needs you don't know about.

To me, banning the mention of specific needs from the pulpit is like saying a breadwinner shouldn't know about specific household bills; he or she should earn a paycheck with a single-minded desire to show love for family. Yet, responding to specific needs is what love is all about. Like the "sheep" (of Matthew 25) who showed their love for Jesus by visiting the sick, feeding the hungry, and clothing the naked, so people in the pew today can show their love for Jesus by responding to specific needs mentioned from the pulpit.

Employ Marketing Principles

I believe God gave marketing principles for the church, not the world. Marketing principles are neither moral nor immoral in themselves. They are tools for reaching worthy goals: to make people aware of our plans, to communicate the importance of those plans, to cast a vision, to communicate a theme, to catch attention and generate interest.

Marketing really means effective communication. Just as farmers need to use the latest agricultural technology just to keep up, so churches need to communicate effectively to keep pace with what people are used to.

During the two months we build up for stewardship month and Loyalty Sunday, we employ a host of marketing principles:

● *Quality.* We don't use some leftover program. Everything is done with excellence. The loyalty committee prints their own quality stationary every year, for example, because people don't take shabbily printed materials or presentations seriously. You can't print flyers on an old mimeograph machine and expect today's people to think your program is well-planned and significant. Our culture has trained people to think that way. The greater the excellence of the publicity and promotion, the greater will be the presumed value of the event.

● *Repetition.* People tend to think what they see the most is the most important. One announcement the week before Loyalty Sunday will not affect people. Neither do two or three announcements do the trick. To communicate the importance of something, people must hear about it weekly for at least five to six weeks. So we start advertising our Loyalty Sunday, which is in early November, the

Sunday after Labor Day.

Publicity doesn't even register until it has been seen several times; people have learned to screen out most of the barrage of advertising they receive every day. One more event at the church will be forgotten unless we fix it in their minds repeatedly.

● *Personal Contact*. United Airlines has a TV ad that pictures a sales meeting headed by an owner upset about losing one of his long-time customers. He thinks it signifies a bigger problem. He tells his sales force that they are going to solve the problem by returning to their former way of doing things.

He walks around the room and hands everyone an airline ticket. Instead of relying on overnight mail, telephones, and fax machines, their company will once again have personal contact with customers. When an employee asks whom he plans to see, the boss replies, "My old friend."

Personal contact makes a difference. We incorporate the human touch into our stewardship campaign. For example, a couple of weeks before Loyalty Sunday, someone from the loyalty committee calls every family in the church, asking which worship service they will attend on Loyalty Sunday, explaining that we will have their packet of materials ready for them.

● *Variety*. This is an aspect of repetition. We communicate in as many forms as possible: letters, phone calls, music, testimonies, children's sermons (which communicate more effectively with the adults than perhaps anything else), posters, skits, overhead transparencies, and banners and signs hung around the facilities. The more forms in which a message is put, the more likely it will connect.

Consider Your Timing

Someone has said that timing is everything. It certainly is for a farmer. His income for the year depends largely on whether he plants at the right time, rains fall at the right time, and fields become dry for harvest at the right time. In church, right actions at the wrong time are just as impotent as wrong actions. Here are some timing factors to take into account.

● *Never spring a special pledge or offering on people.* As I mentioned, we warn at least two months in advance about the pledges to be taken on Loyalty Sunday; we want people to make a prayerful, careful decision. If they do that, over the long haul, they will give more.

If we don't forewarn people, they pledge on their emotions. When that happens, they can't maintain their giving. Then they feel guilty, and since no one likes that, some will stop attending our church.

● *Take current economics into account.* Our church is not pushing for a big increase in pledges for next year. Unemployment in the area now stands at 13 percent. Furthermore, we're raising two million dollars for a building program, and typically such a drive hurts general-fund giving.

Then again, hard times in the economy don't always signal hardscrabble for the church. A decade ago the recession affected us oppositely; our church actually grew in numbers and finances. When hard times strike, people view their lives differently, valuing possessions less and hungering for spiritual things more, and they turn to the church for help. (Sometimes I almost wish, perversely, that the bottom would completely fall out of the economy! As it is, people hold back because they have the financial freedom to buy "toys.")

In either case, I think carefully about what's happening currently in the economy before leading the congregation financially.

● *Move slowly in times of friction.* Staff friction and church factions devastate fund raising. Finances are controversial to begin with; adding fund raising to a church fight spills kerosene on the fire. I take care of first things first: deal with the unrest and then handle the finances.

Similarly, we have found that a bad time to raise funds is when key people leave the staff. Each staff member carries the support of people concerned about that staff member's ministry area. One year we delayed a major construction project because of such a staff change. Waiting a few years restored the sense of peace and joy necessary for members to enthusiastically support a major building-fund drive.

On our Loyalty Sunday, instead of passing plates to receive pledge cards, we ask people to walk to the front and place their pledges on the altar, just as a farmer in Old Testament times would bring the first fruits of his harvest to the temple.

The moment is powerful and symbolic. People of all sorts come forward — wealthy entrepreneurs and the blind, teenagers and those shuffling forward with a walker — all offering the fruit of their labor to the Lord. By allowing people to give in this symbolic manner, it reminds both them and us that we are not just raising a big budget or larger offerings, we are presenting ourselves to the Lord.

*The unified budget will still dominate most churches'
financial structures, but we are wise to recognize this
new financial reality: the rise of designated giving.*

— *Gary Fenton*

CHAPTER SIX

How to Handle
Designated Funds

One man, whose father was a church treasurer, told me how his father's responsibility changed rapidly during the late 1940s and early '50s.

His father had been treasurer for about ten years in a small church. During the ten-year tenure, his task had been primarily to pay the preacher, the custodian, the utility bills, and send money to the denominational office. He kept the church records in a small notebook, with a big rubber band around it, and he stored these records under the bed.

But when the church started to grow, his responsibilities as treasurer changed dramatically. People gave money to furnish the growing nursery, to buy a new organ, and some members began giving to some of the emerging parachurch groups. His father took an accounting class at the local college so he could keep up with the greater complexity.

Gradually, he led the church to put as many of these projects into the central budget as possible. Later he taught treasurers in other local churches how to keep their books.

This, in microcosm, is how the unified budget came into being all across America. It's an accounting system that influenced church giving patterns for many years.

From Unified to Designated Giving

If this chapter had been written twenty years ago, more than likely the content would have been significantly different. The way church leaders and congregations view and use designated gifts has changed radically in the recent past. Following World War II, many church and other charitable organizations discouraged designated giving and encouraged giving to a unified budget: The organization's governing body would structure, budget, and then allocate amounts for the various ministries and programs. The contributors' and donors' gifts would be placed in one fund to support the many ministries.

The movement toward the unified budget in the early 1950s reflected several changes in our culture. First, our nation had just pulled its resources together and experienced a major victory in the war. Pooled resources and energies were one of the major themes our leaders used in interpreting what we had learned during the war. Much of the rhetoric and strategy planning following the war reflected the crisis vocabulary from the 1941–1945 era.

Second, unified giving provided a simple form of bookkeeping. As the soldiers came home from the war, they started families and many churches experienced biological growth. As the story above suggests, that growth led to a more complex financial picture for the church that unified- budget bookkeeping simplified.

Third, denominational leadership began providing training to local church leaders to help organize the large influx of new members after World War II. At the same time, these denominations often encouraged congregations to use unified budgets, since many denominations used them in their national organizations and financial structures. This also helped form a common financial vocabulary among the churches.

Fourth, uniformity was the mood of the 1950s, just as chain stores and franchises, like McDonald's, began sprouting up across the United States. Each local outlet looked like the others, and their employees used the same vocabulary. Denominations became the "chain vendors" in the "religion industry," and uniformity provided the means needed to handle the growing number of "customers." (This analogy is not intended to describe the intent or the motives of the church leaders but merely the process.)

At the local level, all donors were encouraged to contribute to all the major ministries of a congregation. That way, the donor of the smallest gift could participate in the evangelism, education, and mission ministries of their church. It was a great equalizer.

But times are changing, and designated giving — by which people can indicate where specifically in the church their gifts will go — is becoming more and more common, even though churches sometimes deny it! In many churches, leadership reacts strongly against designated giving as if it were an evil. This is especially true in churches who are now being led or have recently been led in financial areas by people trained in the 1950s.

The church I presently serve is in the process of writing some financial policies regarding designated giving. In researching the issue, we discovered that many churches are seeking to update their policies regarding designated giving. Almost all of those we contacted have written policies that discourage designated giving, but several have indicated that their policies in no way reflect their practice.

One large growing church sent us their policy, which specifically stated that they would receive no designated contributions other than to three mission offerings and one other special fund. Yet a review of the church's quarterly financial statement indicated that over forty designated funds were active, covering many different ministries and programs!

We now live in the era of the "designer consumer." Due to a change in technology (which allows for greater choices among consumers) and a new mood, it is important for our people to feel that they are contributing to something they have chosen. Many churches are finding that members are more committed to some ministries and programs than others. Naturally, they like to see their money go to those primarily.

On the other hand, when members find that their designated gifts are discouraged or regarded as less spiritually valid, they may end up giving with less enthusiasm, which continued long enough, may be reduced in quantity as well. In fact, they sometimes find new religious and charitable organizations who will gladly receive their money.

It is a new era in church financing, then. The unified budget will still dominate most churches' financial structures, but we are wise to recognize this new financial reality. Here are some ways I've found to make good use of designated giving.

Remember the Benefits

Having been raised in the unified-budget era, it's easy for me to see the potential problems with designated giving: for instance, it could undermine a sense of church unity, and it could entice individuals to want to control the program or ministry they give to.

No budget system is perfect, and it's important to recognize the weaknesses of any system and shore up the church's defenses at those points. But if I let potential problems with the system preoccupy me, I won't be able to take advantage of the strengths of designated giving. And strengths it has.

● *Designated giving often helps people give their first significant gift.* A successful businessman was feeling quite unsuccessful as a husband and father. He had functioned as a parent the same way as he had as a businessman: he rewarded performance and punished failure. While this worked in his business, it had disastrous results in his family.

Due to a ministry of our church, he experienced a spiritual renewal and began changing this destructive pattern of behavior with his family. Soon he became aware that our church provided a counseling ministry for young families. So he offered a designated gift to the church to underwrite this ministry for one year.

I made an appointment with him to thank him for the gift and to explain that this expense had been budgeted. "We could use your gift as you have indicated," I concluded. "But if you were to give the same generous gift to our budget, you would be able to touch young families for Christ in many ways."

It was not long before he became a regular contributor to the budget. Still, he continued to designate some to the counseling ministry, which allowed us to expand that program.

• *It teaches people the rewards of sacrificial giving.* When people give to a unified budget, it sometimes remains vague as to what they are getting for their money. Designated giving helps people give sacrificially because it shows them what they're getting for their sacrifice. And that one-time sacrifice can blossom into a habit of sacrifice.

A small church that had been static for twenty years purchased a parsonage for their new pastor. The church chose not to put the house payment in the budget and instead proceeded to ask their members to give above their regular offerings to pay off the parsonage. The new pastor brought an excitement and optimism to the congregation, and the church paid off the home in six months. A great amount of excitement had been generated regarding this accomplishment.

The finance committee encouraged the members to continue their giving for six more months, and as a result, a new parking lot was paved and new furniture was purchased for the nursery. Many of the members found they could give and still survive.

At the end of the year-long emphasis, a new budget was presented, and the church budget challenged the congregation to increase its giving by 40 percent in the one year. One of the older members of that congregation says that became a financial breakthrough that forever changed the giving patterns of the church. Although the church paid off their parsonage some twenty years ago, their per capita giving remains one of the highest in their area of the country.

• *Non-urgent ministries are enhanced.* One church I know of has an extensive library and an outstanding collection of audio and video equipment, yet no budget funds are provided for these things. This church completely funds its library and media center through memorial donations.

One of their pastors started this practice after his mother died; he asked members of the church not to send flowers but instead to give to the library. It was not long before people began giving regularly to this library fund.

It is unlikely that any given church will be financially able to make 5 percent of its budget available for something like a library. For some years now, though, this church, which has a budget of approximately $150,000, has received around $7,500 for its library and media center.

Stay in Control of the Gift

As I mentioned, one of the weaknesses of designated giving is that donors may try to control the ministry or program they give to. That can undermine the leaders' authority and become divisive to the church.

I've found ways, however, to check this potential problem.

• *Draw up a policy.* A policy regarding how and when designated giving is received can save a great amount of conflict. The policy can be as simple as this:

"Our church will seek to spend all designated gifts for the purpose the donor desires, as long as that purpose is in keeping with the purposes, policies, and philosophy of the church. If the gift is designated to purchase products or secure special services, the appropriate committee reserves the right to select the vendor or the provider of the services. The designated monies and any item or service purchased with these monies is the property of the church."

This policy can be printed on all receipts for donations or the quarterly contribution statements.

• *Anticipate such gifts.* With increased designated giving, church leaders are wise to anticipate these gifts. During the budget process, the leaders can try to estimate the amount and nature of designated gifts of the coming year. Several key people can often tell church leaders what special ministries and problems interest people.

This can be done in two ways. You can observe what causes and needs are being publicized and promoted in the community. Many churches have begun ministries to the homeless, to the victims of AIDS, and the like in just this way.

The leaders can also recall the causes the pastor has mentioned in his sermons. If a pastor preaches on world hunger or uses an illustration about the homeless that creates some interest, it would not be surprising for, let's say, an evangelized baby boomer to turn that into a flaming passion.

If the church's leaders can discuss the implications of such ministries ahead of actually receiving the gifts, they are in a better position to either turn down the gift or to expedite its use, depending on how the leaders feel about the ministry or program that the giver wants to underwrite.

In addition, if the board is pretty sure that a pressing need will be funded outside the budget in the coming year, it can deliberately fail to fund that ministry and focus its money elsewhere.

Some churches think about what needs the church has and annually publish a list of designated causes that have the approval of their governing body. Such lists anticipate that money will be given and direct that money to the most needy areas of the church.

• *Give donors some choices.* In one small church I served, a family sought to give a $40,000 memorial gift to be placed in a trust, with earnings designated to purchase fresh flowers each Sunday in the worship service. Each Monday, the flowers were to be placed on the graves of the deceased family members of the donor. The donating family had specifically named the florist the church was to use and what color of flowers were to be purchased.

Our memorial committee tactfully declined the offer.

Today, after refusing the gift, I would offer the family other avenues to remember their loved ones. That allows both giver and church to retain some control over their giving.

As mentioned above, many church memorial committees annually identify a half dozen tangible needs that are not in the operating budget and would be appropriate memorials. This not only anticipates giving, it also gives people choices. When people offer an inappropriate memorial, they can be encouraged to consider the other options on the list.

● *Make sure it's deductible.* In one church I served, a man gave money to the pension fund of a staff person nearing retirement. The staff member had served the church nearly thirty years, and for the first twenty the church had provided no retirement benefit. Now the person was edging into his sixties without adequate retirement provision.

An auditor found that this gift was in violation of the IRS regulations, and the donor could not be given a receipt for a tax-deductible gift. The church could correct the inequity, but a donor could not.

One church prevents such potential embarrassment by having a committee review each designated gift. In addition to determining if donors' gifts are in keeping with the philosophy of the church, they also inform donors if the gift can legally become a tax deduction.

Thanking the Giver

Once a church has received a designated gift for an appropriate item, the church needs to thank the donor appropriately and quickly. If it is a memorial gift, then the family of the person in whose memory the contribution was made needs to be notified that a gift has been received.

If our church receives a memorial gift, we send a letter going to both the donor and the family the day after receiving the gift. If I know the gift is going to a ministry or program about which the deceased felt strongly, I mention this in the letter.

This practice is not only simple courtesy, it's also a way to encourage the giver. On several occasions, I have had donors give additional amounts when they realized that the person they were memorializing was deeply involved in the life of the church.

On one occasion an employer gave one hundred dollars to the church's building fund in lieu of sending flowers. Upon receipt of the gift, I sent a letter thanking the company for their contribution, and I mentioned that the deceased had served on the building and grounds committee of the church for several years and had been chairman at the start of the last project.

The employer had not been aware of the man's heavy involvement in the church. Consequently, rather than putting $5,000 in their company's educational trust fund on behalf of the man, as was their custom upon the death of an employee, the employer sent the additional money to the church.

Some churches publicize designated gifts in the church newsletter. If it's a memorial gift, the names of the person in whose memory a gift has been received is also mentioned. One newsletter uses the following statement in their publicity, "Gifts above tithes and weekly budget donations have been given in memory of the following . . ." This not only publicly honors the deceased, it also encourages memorial giving by others.

The Pastor's Role in Memorial Giving

Since the pastor works so closely with the family and friends of the deceased, he or she plays a vital role when a family wants to give a memorial gift. I have found it helpful to follow these practices.

● *Make clear the church's policy on memorial gifts.* When people ask about making a memorial contribution, I immediately send them a letter explaining our church's policy regarding memorial gifts. This prevents some common misunderstandings up front.

A pamphlet we are preparing to put in such a letter will include a list of the ministries and items our memorial committee has identified as especially appropriate for gifts, and explanations of how the church acknowledges memorial gifts and why the church does not attach memorial labels or markers on memorial gifts. This pamphlet will also give the name of the staff member to call if people have further questions.

If the family has asked for suggestions before I've had a

chance to talk with them ahead of time, I'll confer with the memorial committee to find out if what they have determined would be appropriate and then list those in my follow-up letter.

● *Help the family time their giving.* On occasion, I've encouraged the family to wait until a later time to make the memorial gift.

A local pastor ministered to a family who had lost a son in a well-publicized tragedy. Prior to the funeral, the family wanted immediately to establish a memorial fund at the church in memory of the boy. They were willing to make an initial contribution of several thousand dollars and asked the pastor to mention it at the funeral.

The pastor, however, encouraged them to wait. He knew making such a gift would be difficult for the family and would also manipulate the congregation at the funeral. Several months later, the church received a small but more appropriate gift from the family. Although his church could have used the money, the pastor and the church's integrity remained intact.

● *Encourage memorial giving.* Not everyone is tuned into the idea of giving memorial gifts. It's not been a part of their experience, or they've not been aware of what a difference it can make. Since so much good can come from memorial giving, I consider it one of my duties to encourage it.

One way I do this is by taking the honorariums I've received for officiating at funerals and giving them to the church in memory of the deceased. I write the family thanking them for the honorarium and explaining what I have done with it and what types of things their memorial may end up doing for the church. The financial secretary also sends notification to the family that a memorial gift has been given by the pastor in their loved one's memory.

Many people are grateful not only for my gift but also for the idea I've planted in their heads — that the life of their loved one can count for one thing more. That can lead to further gifts that benefit the work of the church.

Designated giving cannot take the place of a good budget, but I doubt that the growing church in the postscript decade to the twentieth century can ignore this funding source. Even though the bulk of funds will remain in a unified budget for years to come, these donor-directed gifts can be used to enhance ministry significantly.

Just as people with the gifts of mercy, music, or leadership need cultivation and sometimes a challenge, so do those with the gift of giving.

— Wayne Pohl

CHAPTER SEVEN

Ministry to Deep-Pocket Donors

In the early stages of a building-fund drive, I asked my secretary to schedule a lunch appointment for me with a church member who had given generously in the past. Three weeks later when we sat together at a local restaurant, I noticed he held in his hand a bundle of envelopes.

He fanned them out on the table and said, "I know why you asked me out to lunch. I hope it's important because lots of requests are coming across my desk." Pointing to the envelopes he said, "These are the appeals I've received since your secretary called."

Competition for the donations of deep-pocket donors is at an all-time high. Ours is a needy world, and thankfully more and more parachurch groups and charities are trying to do something about it. And they have sophisticated fund-raising tools at their disposal: direct mail, telemarketing, telethons and television ads, magazine advertising, radio appeals, candy sales. Unfortunately many Christians, awash in appeals, are on the defensive, especially deep-pocket donors.

How is a pastor supposed to feel about joining the long line at their door? When we get inside, how can we appeal for donations in a way that is both honorable and effective? For me, it begins with perspective.

Deep-Pocket Donors Are a Spiritual Gift

When I look at someone whom God has blessed financially, I don't see a dollar sign, a blank check, a venture capitalist, a bankroll, a cash pipeline. I see the spiritual gift of giving, as mentioned in Romans 12.

I have noticed that these individuals themselves usually see their wealth in the same light. Frequently I hear statements like this: "I am making more money than I ever thought I would make, more money than I think I'm worth to my company. Because God has so richly blessed me, I have to use this money in a way that will benefit other people and God's kingdom."

When I approach someone about giving, I don't see myself as a salesman, a fund raiser, or a beggar. I am the church's leader, charged with the responsibility of training every member to use his or her spiritual gift so that the body might be built up into the image of Christ. As a result of that biblical perspective, I approach deep-pocket givers in the belief that I have the right to do so. So I do it with authority and confidence.

I treat people with the gift of giving just as I treat anyone else. My responsibility is to nurture gifts in the church. Just as people with the gifts of mercy, music, or leadership need cultivation, oversight, and sometimes a challenge, so do those with the gift of giving. Just as I would not hesitate to ask a woman with a strong voice to sing in the church or a carpenter to do repairs, so I don't hesitate to approach people whom God has blessed financially and ask them to support the work of the church.

Nurturing the Gift of Giving

Spiritual gifts aren't used automatically or immediately with expertise. I have found that what I do or don't do dramatically affects how faithfully the people in my church use theirs. This is especially true for those who have the gift of giving.

● *Teach members what your church expects.* One blizzardy night, I found myself in a restaurant crowded with fellow Kiwanians. I couldn't believe I had come out in this blizzard: *This is insane. The authorities are warning everyone to stay off the roads. People don't go out on a night like this.*

Later that night as I drove home through the blowing snow, I came to a STOP sign, and it suddenly hit me: *Kiwanis expects more of their members than the church of Jesus Christ does!* That night, fifteen years ago, I resolved that would not be true in the church I pastor.

We make that clear when we interview and teach new members. If anyone attends our church and expects to do nothing, they're in the wrong place. We teach that giving of ourselves is both an opportunity and a responsibility. We expect members to use their spiritual gifts, and we will help them discover what their gifts are. When we learn how their spiritual gifts can be used, we will ask them to be involved. Because we tell people this up-front, it's not a surprise when we come requesting their involvement.

● *Understand deep-pocket donors' pressures.* Earlier in my ministry, at a time when our denomination was making a special appeal for funds, I received a call from someone on the synodical level who asked me to supply the names of "financially blessed people" in my congregation whom the denomination could contact. The cause was worthy, and I complied.

Later I received a phone call from one of the referrals: "Pastor, I have made clear to you my financial situation, and I have done that willingly. But if you're going to broadcast that around God's whole world, then I will never make such private information known to you again." He viewed my referral as a breach of trust and resented it deeply.

Wealthy people often (and rightly) feel used, as though everyone is after their money. If they think their church is just another place where they will be beat on for their bucks, they won't stay there long.

So asking for donations too often is a mistake. I would not ask someone in our church for an extraordinary gift more than once every five years. I also meet with them for lunch or breakfast when I am not asking for money, showing them I value our relationship, not just their ability to help the church financially.

● *Remember they will give their money elsewhere.* Though deep-pocket donors shouldn't be overasked, neither should they be underasked. When I presented a request for a special church project to one member, he replied, "I wish you had talked to me ten days ago. My wife and I just committed $50,000 to the Detroit zoo!" My thoughts at that moment would not have pleased animal-rights proponents.

Christians with the gift of giving will be naturally inclined to help others. Some charitable group will benefit from their generosity, so it might as well be the church. But if they don't know about the needs and giving opportunities in our church, they won't be inclined to donate to it. Consequently, once a member is established in our congregation, I plant a seed in his or her mind, either by an outright request for a current need or by half-kidding, "When you feel the need to give, we always have an important place to use resources."

● *Match the church's need to their interest.* Several years ago we discussed in our board meeting the idea of purchasing a van to bus people to church, especially elderly people from nursing homes. The van would cost $18,000.

After the meeting, one of the board members came into my office and enthusiastically said, "That Dial-A-Ride ministry is a wonderful idea." One of his elderly relatives, he explained, had been a shut-in for years, unable to attend church.

Two days later, when I came to my office, I found a check on my desk for $9,000 for the van.

I assume Christians believe in the value of our cause and thus don't need me to convince them about the importance of the church, but I do need to help Christians find specific projects that interest them. Generous Christians get excited about giving to different needs. One donor gets excited about foreign missions, another about building churches, another about Bible schools, another about food for the hungry.

My job is to make a full range of giving opportunities available that appeals to various interests. If someone with the gift of giving hasn't yet given, I tell myself that the problem isn't as much theirs as mine: I probably haven't nurtured them enough or presented the need that matches their interest. If I don't touch needs, I don't touch hearts.

• *Be convinced of the necessity of the project.* Deep-pocket givers invariably ask me how important is the project for which I am appealing. A financially successful individual in our congregation, who made a large amount of money in the automotive industry and then started his own business has said to me on numerous occasions, "I am here to help, but I am not here to bail anybody out. I want to do things that nobody else would be able to do. But I have to be convinced that this project is something God wants me to contribute to."

That sentiment is common among deep-pocket donors. So I don't approach them with a steep request unless I am unequivocally convinced (a) that the project is necessary, and (b) that the project is necessary *now*. After all, this individual is probably already tithing and has already pledged for the budget, which supposedly included everything important for the church that year. Any extraordinary requests must have an urgency that prevents us from waiting until next year's budget.

• *Forewarn deep-pocket givers.* No one likes to be blindsided. I don't want deep-pocket donors wondering about ulterior motives, guessing every time I call whether I will be asking for money. I prevent that by being upfront about my intentions. When my secretary calls for an appointment, she informs them that I want to present them with a proposal.

A forewarning helps deep-pocket givers by affording them time to consider any objections and then discuss them with me.

When I presented an appeal to one man, he said, "I have done a lot for the church over the years. I think it's time for some of the younger guys to do their part. For the good of the program, I want to hold back."

I was able to convince him that we needed him as a model for the younger guys! By forewarning him, though, I gave him time to process his feelings, and then I could address them. That prevented later misgivings.

● *Respond gracefully if they say no.* I don't strong-arm the reluctant. If someone says no to my request, I don't want to leave them with a bad taste in his or her mouth. I want to nurture people as long-term givers. A short-term, hard-sell approach, worrying only about the church's current need, will only undermine future giving.

A businessman in our church who is worth millions responded to one of my appeals by explaining, "Right now I'm not sure week to week whether we're even going to make payroll. I've never been this tight with the dollar in my life." I don't argue with valid objections. Many people wealthy on paper have investments that cannot be easily liquidated, such as real estate. Though worth millions, they can't come up with $5,000.

I receive their refusals gracefully and don't labor the point, aware that they may feel guilty or embarrassed. Typically I will respond, "I respect your honesty and know that you do what you can for our church. I will pray and trust that the Lord will improve your situation, so don't be surprised when eventually I ask you again. God is doing something special in our church. If God blesses you in the future, and you want to help, don't wait for me to call."

When do I stop coming back? Only when I feel a person is trying to get rid of me. If that's the case, then I'm not helping them.

After They Give

Our nurturing and caring for donors after they give is just as important as motivating them to give in the first place. Giving a large gift raises a person's interest in, commitment to, and feelings for the church. Many can be easily offended if they feel the church does not respond or follow through properly.

On the other hand, if the entire experience is positive and they truly experience what the Scripture promises — that it is more blessed to give than to receive — then they will look forward to giving again. I believe that deep-pocket donors will continue to enjoy giving if we do three things well.

● *Recognize the gift.* A man in our church owns a successful furniture company. For several years his wife Mary Lee worked as bookkeeper in our church office. Bookkeeping having become a major job due to the size of our congregation, Mary Lee often said, "I wish we could get computers at church like the ones we have in business."

We began researching various computer systems for our situation, which were just beginning to come on the market, and they were extremely expensive, about $30,000.

Sometime later Mary Lee learned she had cancer. Eventually she died. Her husband wanted to buy something for the church in her memory, so I told him what she had often said about the computer system. He welcomed the idea immediately.

Months later, on the first day our new system was up and running, I printed out some of our work and mailed it to him with a note: "We didn't realize how much we would appreciate your gift in Mary Lee's name until today. Now we know. As you can see, this is really going to help our ministry. Most important of all, God knows what you did."

Since then he annually comes into our office and asks us what would be needed to upgrade the system; then he tells us to buy whatever it takes to do that and send him the bill. Over the years he probably has invested over $100,000 in our computers.

When people use their spiritual gifts in a special way in the church, I mail them thank-you notes. It's no different when people give special monetary gifts to the church. In the note I remind givers of what good will result from their gifts, affirm their ultimate motives for giving — to serve Christ and his kingdom — and remind them of the church's gratitude.

I don't, however, recognize such gifts from the pulpit, and we're not enthusiastic about nailing plaques to everything in the church. In my experience, generally the larger the gift, the less the donor wants it known. Most often the one condition set by deep-pocket donors is that no one knows about their contribution but me. They don't give to impress others, and sometimes they are concerned about attracting a line of people at their door, hat in hand. For a building program, we list donors in a book.

● *Inform them of the status of a purchase.* We recently bought a new church sign toward which one couple, Mike and Clara, contributed significantly. We chose to work with a company based in the South, which had to fly a representative into Detroit to confer with us, so the job took a lot longer than anticipated. Throughout the long process, we updated Mike and Clara, who had no trouble understanding the delays. When the sign finally stood in place, although glitches and frustrations had to be overcome in the process, everyone was happy.

When people invest heavily in a project, they "own" it. It's important to them. And when they own it, they wonder how it's progressing, imagine how it will look, perhaps worry that everything will be done right. These are natural feelings that we are wise to respect.

If significant problems with a project arise, I communicate that to the donor immediately and forthrightly. Deep-pocket givers usually work with movers and shakers, doers and shooters, people who see right through a snow job. Honest communication is extremely important to them. They will understand difficulties; they will not understand being ignored or misled.

● *Properly allocate the gift.* With our church in the middle of a building program, we were feeling intense cash-flow pressure. People were shifting their giving to the building, so the general fund was down. Meanwhile the local economy was in deep doldrums, leaving lots of people unemployed. One Sunday I mentioned in my sermon the needs of many in our congregation.

The next Sunday one man approached me after the service

and said, "My wife and I have been praying about what you said last week. I have a check here for $15,000. I want the church to divide it among members with needs."

At that moment my feelings were mixed. Part of me was rejoicing that we could help those who were hurting. Another part of me, feeling the church's financial pressure, was thinking, *Why didn't I preach on something else last Sunday?* That may not have been the right sentiment, but that's what I felt.

Nevertheless, no matter the pressure, a pastor can't think for a moment about reallocating designated money. Misallocating funds is not only immoral; it's suicide. If a congregation ever learns that money has been reallocated without congregational or donor approval, trust is gone.

Control also can become an issue. A husband and wife once said to the chairman of our music department, "The church's piano looks a bit tacky. Does the church need a new one?"

Bill, our music director, replied, "We sure do."

"Shop around and see what is available," the potential deep-pocket giver said.

Bill visited various piano showrooms, researching until he found what he felt would be the best piano for us. It happened to be manufactured in Japan.

When he informed the potential donors of what he wanted to buy, they said, "That's not American made."

Bill said, "No, but it's the best piano for our church."

This long-time resident of Detroit made it clear that he would not donate to the church for a foreign-made product. Bill later came into my office and asked, "What are we going to do about this?"

Normally a person designates what they want their gift to buy. In theory their control ends there. In practice, however, we want donors to be happy with their contribution.

Well-acquainted with Detroit values, I decided that though our music director wanted a different piano, the sentiments of many more people than the donor would be rubbed raw by a foreign-made purchase, so I said, "Go back through the sales materials and find the best American-made piano for our church."

At that point nurturing a person's gift of giving and respecting community values was more important than a particular piano. At other times we exert more leadership, but in a way that still nurtures the giver.

For example, people love to give to the music program (by now we could have forty sets of handbells). When someone offers to buy handbells or some other unneeded product, we leave the decision to them but frankly say, "You can buy handbells for the church if you want, but they won't be used. We already have more than one set. Let me suggest another place to contribute where we have a greater need."

Going Outside the Fold

Our church sponsors a food ministry called St. Paul Pantry, which is well-known in our community. Although it can be a drain on workers — we receive calls day and night and the community refers hundreds of people annually — we do it because we feel led of the Lord. People in the community don't care why we run St. Paul Pantry, but they do see the benefits and often call to offer financial support.

We don't require people to sign a doctrinal statement to contribute to our ministry. If the community benefits — for example, from an athletic program or a building that is used regularly for community-wide programs — I will not only accept donations but invite them. We inform potential donors up front about our philosophy of ministry and our spiritual purposes, show them how the community will be enhanced, and welcome their support.

We sponsor a classical concert series each year, the best in the area, for the purpose of reaching new people for Christ. The series has been so fruitful that the church would underwrite it completely, but people want to be patrons. One of our members worked in the office of three successful dentists, and she invited them to the concerts. They attended and since have contributed heavily each year. Their help and that of others frees us to use general funds for other purposes.

One of our men came into my office and said, "Pastor, some of the sanctuary walls are fading. Why don't you get an estimate for a paint job?"

Our director of buildings and church properties took bids, and the best offer was $14,000. When I informed our potential deep-pocket donor, he wrote out a check for $14,000 and said, "Tell the contractors I'd like it done by Easter."

The first Sunday after the painters finished the job, I saw him walk into our early service, lift his eyes to the walls and ceiling, look behind the radiator, and smile.

And that made me smile. Because when deep-pocket donors give and smile, keep giving and keep smiling, they have fulfilled their calling — and I, part of mine.

Too often churches, because they are communities of faith built upon trust, inadvertently place opportunities for temptation in front of their members.

— Richard L. Bergstrom

CHAPTER EIGHT

Where Churches Are Vulnerable

At the annual meeting of Euzoa Bible Church on October 8, 1985, our 42-year-old youth pastor, who had been with the church eight years, stood before the congregation and read the following confession:

I have sinned against God, my wife, my children, my family, and the body of Christ here at Euzoa. For almost six years I have been stealing from the general offerings of this church. I have taken cash and checks and deposited them into the youth checking account. I then wrote checks for cash on that account and used the money for personal use. I have lied to many of you and have deceived you. The depth of the deception is so ingrained, I do not know the amount of my stealing. I am dependent upon the elders and their audit to know the scope of my sin.

Further, I have not filed federal or state income tax for eight years. While my wife knew of my failure to file with the IRS, I hid the extent of the shambles of our personal finances from her. She persisted in praying that I would be responsible and from time to time attempted to confront me with questions regarding our financial affairs. But I lied to her, and she, because of her trust, accepted my lies.

I have been moved to confess my sin through the fear of God, through fear of the growing pressure and presence of the IRS, and through fear of being found out. God has also used Pastor Dick, who became aware of problems in our finances and persisted in seeking to love and help me.

Mine are the sins of stealing, lying, and deceit. Those are the symptoms of a deeper sin of a lack of trusting God and a lack of inner discipline. I have asked God, my wife and family, and the board of elders for forgiveness. And I ask you to forgive me.

I have not only sinned against you but have broken the law. Since I have committed a felony against you and the people of this state by my sin, I will be meeting with the district attorney, giving a full confession of my crime.

In reading this confession, I hereby resign from all pastoral positions and responsibility. I submit to the authority of the elders and to the civil authorities of this nation for God's discipline through them.

Alan's confession marked the anniversary of my first year of ministry at Euzoa Bible Church — and the worst tragedy of my ministerial career.

A year earlier, in May of 1984, I had asked my wife, "What did I do with that letter from the church in Colorado?"

"It's under the bed," she replied.

One phone call led to another and to a stop in Steamboat Springs for a brief interview while I was on vacation in June. We saw some tremendous obstacles to successful ministry in this independent church in a resort community. Yet within a few months, we found ourselves in a U-Haul traveling from the Pacific Northwest to northwest Colorado.

We had some concerns about the youth pastor, who had been open about his desire to be senior pastor. I was told, however, that Alan (not his real name) was a unique individual who would be able to accept whatever decision the church made. One person had mentioned in passing that Alan had some problems with his personal finances, but "nothing that important." I was assured it had been taken care of by the church boards.

I learned later that Alan had been three months delinquent on his rent, for which he had been given a rental allowance by the church. The church's solution had been to begin paying his rent directly to the landlord, thus "solving" the problem.

Within a month after coming to Euzoa, however, I began to sense something wrong. For the previous eight years, Alan had been having his mail delivered to the church post office box. In the process of sorting it out, I couldn't help noticing the pattern of notices of late payments, intents to shut off gas and electrical service, and pink slips indicating overdrafts from the local bank.

"How can he get away with that in a town as small as Steamboat?" I asked my wife.

By the third month, I was bothered enough to raise the issue with the person who had alluded to Alan's financial problems before I came. He assured me he would look into it further, but nothing developed.

By the sixth month, I felt a confrontation with Alan was in order. When I asked him about his personal financial situation, he struggled as he talked.

"We had a lot of unanticipated expenses following my mother-in-law's funeral in California," he finally replied. Indeed, they'd had to drop everything to attend her funeral in California — and that just after they had vacationed there in late August. I decided to take his explanation at face value.

Nevertheless, the pattern continued. I began to document the steady stream of bad mail. But I questioned my own motives: *Hadn't Alan tried to be senior pastor? Am I trying to bring about his demise so he is not a threat to my own leadership?* I began to wonder if he should get another mailbox so I wouldn't have to see the notices.

Perhaps most troublesome were the overdrafts. According to my experience, each of those pink slips represented a twelve-dollar expense charged against one's account. *How can he afford such neglect?* I asked myself.

Then another question occurred to me, *I wonder if Alan gets as many pink slips for the church's youth fund? If he can't manage his personal account, what about church funds?* Yet, I couldn't challenge his integrity without damaging our relationship. The church was in the process of revising its entire accounting structure, but to this point, no one had brought the youth fund into the church's general accounting process. When I asked about it, I was told, "Alan handles that."

Failing to get answers through the official channels, and with Alan evasive when I tried to confront him, I decided to look for myself.

In July 1985, I opened the bank statement from the church's youth fund. I found no notices of overdrafts, but I was perplexed. I began to make notations on a three-by-five card. My index card soon couldn't hold all the data. I gathered up as many of the checking account statements as I could find, and later at home, I took out a legal pad and began to go through them one by one. To my amazement, I found from October 1982 to July 1985 a total of $17,792.00 in checks made out to *Cash*, written for *even amounts*, and signed by Alan.

I listed my questions, including

— How are these accounted for?

— Where are the receipts for auditing purposes?

— How do funds get *into* this account — from young people's fees for activities or from the church budget?

— Do youth fees (if collected) cover all or part of the youth outings or events?

— What percentage does the church cover?

— Why are these checks always in round figures (youth expenses obviously aren't)?

— What, then, was done with the change?

— Does anybody hold the youth pastor accountable for monies spent?

I struggled long into the night with the biggest question: *What do I do with the information?* I knew well what asking such questions would mean to our relationship, whether or not there was a legitimate explanation. I knew the biblical principles for church discipline that suggest individual confrontation, but based on Alan's lack of receptivity to my inquiry into personal finances, I doubted whether another personal conversation would be fruitful.

I also knew that 1 Timothy 5 said not "to entertain an accusation against an elder unless it is brought by two or three witnesses. Those who sin are to be rebuked publicly, so that the others may take warning." To bring accusation against someone who had made his livelihood from the ministry for the last twenty years was no small matter. I decided I needed more facts.

I took my findings the next day to the chairman of our church board. He was as puzzled as I.

"What do you make of it?" I asked.

"Well, if the IRS saw this, Alan would be required to pay personal income tax on these amounts unless he has a record of how the money was spent."

"We need to get some answers to where this money came from and how it is being spent," I suggested, "but I'm just not certain how to go about it."

We agreed to ask the trustees to call for an accounting of the youth fund in preparation for a possible move to handling youth ministry expenses through the church's general accounting structure. The rationale would be that all other aspects of the church's finances were being reviewed, so why not the youth fund?

In the meantime, I asked the church financial secretary to document deposits from the general fund into the youth account over the last year. Her findings suggested no inordinate amounts of money going into the youth fund. Where then was that money coming from?

For the next two months, the investigation was put on hold as I was consumed by an assignment to rewrite the church constitution and restructure the ministry under a single board of elders. On September 8, with a full house, the church approved the constitution with a 77 percent vote. In addition, the combined boards of the church proposed a major fund-raising program to build a new building on the three acres of land owned by the church. We planned to present the proposal at our October 8 meeting, after which the new constitution, with an elder board, would go into effect.

During September, however, Alan began getting letters from the IRS.

"Now what kind of trouble is he in?" I commented to my wife. "Not only does he fail to pay his bills but also the tax man is after him!"

"How can he possibly be considered as an elder with that kind of reputation?" she asked. Her question lodged in my soul. Indeed, I had been teaching and preaching on the biblical qualifications of eldership all summer. Is it possible to exclude a staff pastor from an eldership role? Our new structure would have allowed for such a scenario, but did I dare suggest such a distinction for a man, 42 years old, with twenty years in the ministry? It would seem like a power play.

When the third letter in as many weeks arrived from the IRS, I knew I had to have some answers. I called Alan to see if I could come to his home. The events of the next few days were to read like Sergeant Friday's entries in a *Dragnet* episode.

Wednesday, October 2: "Alan, I've noticed for some time that you've been in financial difficulty. And now you're getting notices from the IRS. Are you in trouble?"

Icy silence.

"Alan, I merely want to know how we can help you. If you're in deep trouble financially, we need to be aware of that."

He was quiet. Then he told me he had gotten behind in paying his taxes a few years back but that he had sought advice from a lawyer in the community and was working on getting it straightened out. I asked for permission to get a progress report from the lawyer. He said no.

My confidence in Alan's trustworthiness and willingness to make himself accountable to the church had deteriorated.

Friday, October 4: I met with the chairman of my board for an update on the youth fund investigation, and he informed me he had passed the matter on to the trustees, as we had decided in July. He did not know what the current status of the investigation was. I told him about the recent IRS letters.

Saturday, October 5, 5 P.M.: My concern was growing as we approached the annual meeting and the appointment of elders. I talked with one of the financial officers of the church, and for the first time, he saw the hard evidence. Regarding the IRS situation, he said that "Alan could work out his personal financial situation without it affecting his relationship to the church."

What about the youth fund questions? With two years of documentation on a yellow legal pad in front of him, he said, "Alan would never do anything wrong. And anyway, that's past, and there's nothing we can do about it. Let's not overreact."

I left feeling all alone. I couldn't understand why no one else sensed the magnitude of the information I possessed. But I couldn't stop now.

Saturday, October 5, 7:30 P.M.: After sitting nervously through a birthday dinner for my wife, I met with two deacons in the back room of the parsonage and spilled out my concerns. By this time, I was convinced the circle of awareness had to be expanded. For the first time, the term *embezzlement* was suggested by one of the men. They determined that the rest of the deacon board had to be brought into the discussion. A meeting was scheduled for Sunday, immediately after the service.

Sunday, October 6, 11 A.M.: The bell in the church tower rang out over Steamboat Springs as it had for the past ninety-four years. I had Alan open the service with the call to worship — Isaiah 55:6–7: "Seek the Lord while he may be found; call on him while he is near. Let the wicked forsake his way and the evil man his thoughts. Let him turn to the Lord, and he will have mercy on him, and to our God, for he will freely pardon."

What Alan did not realize at the time was that my wife had prayerfully selected the passage in hopes that God would use it to bring Alan to a point of confession. He seemed emotionally gripped during the reading, barely able to make it through the passage.

Sunday, October 6, 12:30 P.M.: The deacons met in closed session after morning worship to hear the report from the two men with whom I had spent Saturday evening. I did not attend. I greeted people as they left the church but kept fearing the consequences if my suspicions were wrong.

Sunday, October 6, 4 P.M.: At the request of the deacons, I asked Alan to be present at a meeting immediately following the evening service. He hesitantly said he would come.

Sunday, October 6, 7:30 P.M.: We stood waiting for the arrival of one deacon. Alan seemed nervous. I tried to console him — "It's going to be okay. We just want to talk with you."

He said softly, "I'm about to do the second most difficult thing in my life: to meet with you all. And then I'm going to do the most difficult thing: to meet with my family."

Ten minutes later, as we continued to wait for the latecomer, Alan was at the end of his emotional endurance. "Can we get started, fellows?" he asked.

Just then our missing board member arrived. We sat down to begin the meeting, and Alan immediately assumed the floor and proceeded to spill the guilt of six years of stealing directly from the church offering plates.

One-by-one around the table, our heads were lowered into our hands. We had called the meeting to ask Alan about his personal financial problems. We weren't prepared for what we had to hear. We silently prayed for mercy.

We agreed to meet the next night to determine our response.

Monday, October 7: The board of deacons met for the last time. The next day, they would be called "elders." Little did they know when they agreed to serve that they would be tried by fire so soon in their new office.

We mapped out how this information would be shared with the congregation. We determined to hold the annual meeting as scheduled, followed by a public reading of confession by Alan. His resignation would then be voted on by the congregation.

Tuesday, October 8: Alan read his confession at the annual meeting of Euzoa Bible Church.

Before proceeding with the rest of the story, perhaps it would be helpful to analyze the painful lessons we learned about church finances.

The Holes in the System

We had thought the church's financial accountability systems were adequate. After all, the church was careful to insure that separate parties were required to (1) record funds and report receipts and balances monthly (the financial secretary), (2) authorize payment (the trustee board), and (3) write checks (the treasurer). Great pains were taken to reconcile any differences in the records. Written warrants were required for all checks. Any checks for more than $1,000 required two signatures.

But some large holes remained in the financial structures of our church. These holes, I discovered after conversations with other pastors, often exist in other churches' systems, too.

The holes exposed at Euzoa were:

1. The church held two morning services, and the offerings from the first service would be collected and placed in the room behind the pulpit, *uncounted* and *unattended.* The offering room, though just off the platform, had a rear entrance to which Alan had access.

Following the second service, the offerings would then be counted and placed in a deposit bag and left in the night depository at the bank. The next morning the financial secretary would go to the bank and record the receipts.

2. Even if we had counted the first service offering immediately, our system would still have had a hole. The Sunday counting procedure included only the *cash.* It was assumed that *checks* were not

vulnerable, but they were, since they could be "officially" endorsed into a bogus account.

3. The church did not issue annual receipts for giving, unless requested by the individual. It was assumed the canceled checks were all the receipt necessary.

4. The church allowed individual ministry funds to exist in the church's name with *no required accounting* and *no auditing*, in this case, for eight years.

5. The church allowed an employee to have sole authority to write checks against a corporate fund.

(Though gaping, these are not the only holes that exist within the accounting structures of many churches. One substantial hole many churches suffer is to allow one individual to bag up the day's receipts and take them home to count and record. The practice remains in many congregations because challenging such procedures seems an affront to the individual's integrity.)

Using and Abusing the System

With the opportunity before him, Alan employed the following procedures to divert church funds for his own needs:

1. In addition to the "Euzoa Youth Fund," Alan set up a separate account for the "Euzoa Youth Fellowship Fund." Thus there were two youth funds in the church's name — one for legitimate youth funds and activities, and another through which church offerings could be laundered.

2. He would take checks directly out of the offering plates between services or during the second service. I remembered many Sundays seeing Alan leave during the middle of a service and return later on. At the time, I assumed he was checking on the nursery or children's church — not an unusual procedure for a youth pastor.

3. He would then stamp the back of the checks with EUZOA BIBLE CHURCH — FOR DEPOSIT ONLY, blocking out the general account number and depositing them in the Youth Fellowship Fund. Individuals would thus receive their canceled checks with EUZOA BIBLE CHURCH clearly stamped on the back. Because no annual giving

receipts were provided, no one suspected the funds were not going to the designated accounts.

4. Having deposited the funds into the bogus youth account, Alan was then free to write checks with no questions asked.

5. When questions were asked from time to time by the trustees, Alan was able to provide a clean accounting of the "official" Euzoa youth fund.

Our experience reveals one glaring weakness many churches face: namely, that if an individual can access checks *and* set up a separate account in the name of the church, it is then within that person's reach to divert church funds. Of course, cash can be pocketed without the fuss.

Our situation was complicated by the fact that a fund existed in the name of the church that the church did not even know about. This was made easier by the fact that we are situated in a smaller community where things may be more informal than in a larger city. Someone in a position of trust, such as a minister, is often able to convince bank personnel to override policies.

I was troubled enough about the matter to ask two local bank officials about it. "Do you mean, if I came into your bank and asked to open a checking account in a corporate name, you would do that without a letter of authorization from the corporation?" Their response:

1. A corporate account initially requires a form to be filled out and placed on file with the bank. It provides "the authorization of a corporation to maintain a deposit account." In some cases, a single document may authorize a host of accounts under one umbrella, all supposedly on record with the bank. In other cases, a bank may require an authorization letter for every account opened under that corporate name.

2. It is the responsibility of the corporation to provide the bank with a list, updated annually, of persons authorized to sign checks on corporate accounts. If it fails to do this, former employees or corporate officers may be able to continue to write checks against corporate accounts without any indication of wrongdoing.

3. Any new accounts opened under the corporation's name ought

to have a signed letter of authorization before that account is opened by the bank. However, it is conceivable that the same person opening the account could be authorized to sign such a form — or could easily forge the signature of a corporate officer without raising undue suspicions.

That means anyone, potentially, could go into a bank and open an account in the name of the church. Then, any check not immediately recorded and secured is vulnerable. Specific examples of such points of vulnerability would be:

● A member is handed a check by a parishioner and told to put it in the offering plate because the parishioner is not able to be at the service.

● A secretary receives checks in the mail from absent or out-of-town donors.

● A counter is left alone with church funds.

● An usher takes the offering plate to the counting room alone.

In one church, an ingenious usher slid bills out of the top offering plate and stashed them in a bottom plate as he went to the counting room. Then, as he returned the "empty" plates to the storage cupboard, he would recover the bills.

These scenarios are not offered to create a climate of suspicion in churches but to point out that financial irresponsibility can take many guises.

How We Closed the Holes

As a result of the crisis, we took several steps that otherwise would have been difficult to take. But I'm convinced they are worth taking even without such a precipitating event, since they help churches insure their financial integrity.

First, we began to place the filled offering plates on the table in front of the church for all to see. In many churches, an immediate counting in a secured room is more practical and just as effective. In our case, we felt a public demonstration of our accountability was in order.

Second, a new schedule of counters was drawn up. Two individuals were required to be present at all times when offerings were handled and counted. Two signatures were required on the counters' sheet.

Third, two copies of the counting sheet were completely filled out and signed by the counters. One was included in the bank deposit bag for the financial secretary, and one was given to the pastor.

Fourth, all separate church checking accounts (women's fellowship, benevolence fund) were brought under the general accounting structure of the church. We required them to be balanced monthly by the church treasurer. A better option may be to have *no* separate checking accounts but to have all funds handled through a central account.

Fifth, we began issuing annual receipts for giving to all contributors.

Sixth, all local charge accounts that would not supply individual receipts with their monthly invoices were closed. It became impossible to monitor charge accounts that did not provide this service. We suspected that abuses had taken place with the church's grocery store account.

Seventh, all ministry heads or program leaders were made accountable for the expenditures within their budget areas. They were required to sign all requests for payments before the finance committee received them. The effect was to give responsibility for monitoring the budget back to the program chairpersons. Though cumbersome at times, we chose this as an alternative to a single purchasing agent or an advance purchase order system.

A Matter of Trust

The above measures may seem extreme. They were not for us. A sacred trust had been violated. Confidence needed to be restored.

For the first months following the public disclosure, no one, including myself, wanted to be seen holding the church's money or left alone in a room with it. We were almost paranoid about someone suspecting us of wrongdoing. The extreme measures were taken to restore confidence in the system *and* to assure those who handled church finances that they were beyond suspicion.

As a result of aggressive reform and complete openness before our church body, the level of stewardship did not decline but rather increased after the embezzlement problem had been cleared up.

Too often churches, because they are communities of faith built upon trust, inadvertently place opportunities for temptation in front of their members or their ministers. No system is beyond abuse, but responsible stewardship demands church finances be handled with absolute integrity.

Epilogue

On October 8, 1985, following Alan's confession, the congregation voted to accept his resignation but not to press charges against him for his crimes.

Two days later, officers of the church reported the crime to the Colorado district attorney's office, according to their legal obligation as fiduciaries of corporate accounts (Sec. 18-8-115 of the Colorado Criminal Code: "Duty to report a crime-liability for disclosure").

On December 24, Alan was charged with thirteen counts of felony theft and two counts of misdemeanor theft. Each felony charge represented a period of six months in which more than $200 but less than $10,000 was stolen. Each carried a possible jail sentence of one to eight years in the state correctional system, and a maximum fine of $500,000.

On April 1, 1986, Alan pleaded guilty to four counts of class IV felony theft. A month later, Alan was sentenced to thirty days in the Routt County Jail and four years of probation. As required by the courts, but not by Euzoa Bible Church, he was to begin making restitution of $41,857.35 of stolen church funds.

Five months later, Euzoa Bible Church received official notification from the IRS that Alan owed $84,357.02 in unpaid taxes, penalties, and interest for the years 1978–1986.

The judge, upon reviewing Alan's financial condition, did not enforce the requirement that restitution be made, due to an "inability to pay." The IRS continues, however, to garnish the wages of Alan's family to repay back taxes, penalties, and interest.

In May 1990, Alan completed his four years of supervised probation. During that time, Alan had remained in the community and under the discipline of the elders of Euzoa Bible Church. He willingly complied with the conditions set forth for restoration to the fellowship of the church. He and his family have continued as active members of the church, where Alan teaches a Sunday school class and leads a home Bible study.

The fatal mistake of many pastors and churches is to assume that they and those around them are above financial temptation.

— Richard L. Bergstrom

CHAPTER NINE

Insuring Financial Integrity

I t was six years to the day after my youth pastor in Colorado had confessed to eight years of embezzling church funds (my wife remembers the date well — it was on her birthday), and I was dealing with a major dilemma. We had just concluded a pastors' conference through our ministry with Church Dynamics, and I was trying to decide what to do with the funds.

We had received $180 in cash and $200 worth of checks made out to CHURCH DYNAMICS INTERNATIONAL. I needed to reimburse myself for $180 in expenses incurred, and I owed $90 to the woman who had prepared the food for the day. I conferred with our staff, and we decided it would be easiest to set up a conference account locally and keep the funds separate for future conferences in the Northwest.

When I got home, it hit me: *If I were to do that, I would face the same temptations that befell my youth pastor fourteen years ago when he set up a separate youth account in the name of the church!* A cold chill ran down my spine as I realized how much I had forgotten in the previous six years.

A quick mental review brought the lessons of the past to mind. If I were to have a separate fund in the corporate name of our ministry, I had to assume I would be tempted to mingle ministry and personal funds and justify reimbursements to myself that might otherwise be considered out-of-pocket expenses.

For example, as I filled up my gas tank for the return trip home, I wondered, *Should I pay for this, or should the ministry? After all, I came to the conference at my own expense.* My mind tried to justify turning in an expense voucher to the conference account, but my heart knew better.

I also realized I would be tempted to deposit other checks in the corporate name that would be accessible to me. Both individuals and churches occasionally send us support checks made out to CHURCH DYNAMICS INTERNATIONAL, which are intended to go to our ministry headquarters, where a deduction is taken out that goes to the larger ministry. Depositing them locally would save me that deduction and further the local ministry. How logical. How improper!

And even if I weren't subject to any of the above temptations, it would leave me open to accusation if there were ever any discrepancies in the account balance. In order to avoid any problems, I decided to send the funds to our ministry headquarters for processing.

Churches and ministers regularly face similar sticky situations. As we make decisions about how to insure integrity in such situations, I've found that several principles need to be kept in mind.

Original Sin Is Alive and Well

If I learned anything through that gut-wrenching experience six years ago, it was that none of us are above abuse of funds. The only way to protect oneself and others is not to provide the opportunity in the first place. The fatal mistake of many pastors and churches is to assume that they and those around them are above such temptations:

— "It could never happen here. All these precautions are just not worth the effort."

— "Margaret has been doing our church finances for thirty years. She would never take any of the church's money."

— "Fred is the largest contributor in our church. He wouldn't have any reason to divert church funds."

— "Others know I can be trusted with church funds. I don't need to keep detailed records."

Over the years, I've heard many people share their stories. Somewhere along the line I lost count of the incidents reported, but here are a few examples that indicate how wrong such assumptions can be:

— In Colorado, a layman told me how a man in his congregation volunteered to set up the church's finances on computer. Before the board figured out what was going on, he had skipped town with over $60,000, leaving his family behind.

— In Arizona, an usher bilked a church out of $100,000 before being nabbed in an FBI sting, which passed marked bills through the offering.

— In Southern California, a trusted layman diverted over $200,000 of the church's building fund into unauthorized investments for personal gain — and then lost the entire amount. The church lost their financial credibility, and he went to jail over the matter.

— In Colorado, a pastor was fired when it was discovered he was using a secondary account to make personal purchases and pay seminary tuition, which was not the intended use of the fund. Today he's a salesman.

— In the Midwest, a layman inadvertently lost a large sum of money designated for the church's building fund when he made an investment that went sour. Because the investment had not been authorized by the church, he faced criminal charges. Other church leaders stepped in to cover the loss and avoid criminal prosecution.

We really should know better. The Bible is clear about our sinful natures. Even though saved, all of us still struggle with the temptations of the world, the flesh, and the devil.

"The heart is deceitful above all things," says the prophet Jeremiah, "who can know it?" (Jer. 17:9). The author of Proverbs writes, "Who can say, 'I have kept my heart pure; I am clean and without sin'?" (Prov. 20:9). And the apostle John reminds us that "If we claim to be without sin, we deceive ourselves and the truth is not in us" (1 John 1:8).

Given this reality, we have little choice but to take steps to insure financial integrity in our ministries.

Personal Financial Stability of Leaders Helps

The more stable the financial lives of church leaders, the more likely it is that they will maintain integrity in handling church finances. It was problems in his personal finances, among other factors, that led my youth pastor to embezzle church funds.

Scripture is replete with admonitions to insure the financial integrity of the church's leaders, insisting that such people be "blameless" — "not pursuing dishonest gain," "not a lover of money," and having "a good reputation with outsiders."

There's a reason for that. I've observed that even an essentially honest person can become vulnerable to mismanaging corporate funds if he or she suffers a job layoff, a business failure, limited income in retirement years, or a catastrophic health problem. When the circumstances of a person's life change that dramatically, the pressures can be enormous. That's why I feel it is important to know about an individual's financial status before asking him or her to handle the church's funds.

How you discover that, of course, is not easy. How people use their money is a private matter. One can never be sure what's going on behind the scenes, but we are wise to look for the following indicators before letting someone handle the church's funds:

• *A generous pledge to the church.* Many churches require that their leaders be faithful tithers. "We expect that if people are going to be leaders in the church, they will be modeling faithful steward-ship in their lives," says one pastor. "We don't monitor the average layperson's giving with the same degree of scrutiny. But we do expect lay leaders to be tithers to their local church."

• *Up-to-date on all pledge payments.* If a person is behind in pledge payments, it may indicate either an unwillingness to follow through on commitments or a personal financial shortfall. In either case, churches are wise to ask why the payments are not up-to-date.

By the way, tracking pledges not only helps choose good leaders, it's also one way the pastor can stay in touch with the personal lives of the church's leaders.

One pastor I know reviews the tithe statements of all pastoral staff and elders. He does this to note if giving drops — that may indicate either a financial or a spiritual problem.

"People often vote with their wallet before they vote with their feet," says the pastor. "This way, we can discover problems immediately and deal with them."

If a problem is revealed, the pastor or one of the elders seeks out the individual and asks how the church can help. Perhaps the person has incurred unexpected expenses or has lost his job but is too proud to turn to the church for help.

• *No hint of reputation as a free spender.* One member from a previous ministry came home one day with a new truck, without ever discussing the purchase with his wife. For him, spending money like this was a way to assert himself over a domineering wife. It pointed to a much deeper need in his life as well as his marriage, which later ended in divorce. He was not the kind of person to whom I wanted to entrust the church's finances.

• *A good reputation in the community.* My last pastorate was in a small community where the leading men and women prided them-selves on being good lawyers, physicians, salespersons, and business people, and many of these people came to our church. The atmosphere nearly demanded that the church's financial leaders be solid people with healthy reputations in their life and work.

But no matter the community, a church cannot have a lay leader who has a shady business reputation making an appeal for the offering.

A good reputation doesn't necessarily mean, however, a reputation for financial success. People can maintain a strong reputation even in the midst of financial adversity.

I worked with one lay leader whose business failed due to circumstances beyond his control. For a long time he had creditors hounding him to pay overdue bills.

Through the entire experience, however, the church board stood by him; all the other parts of his life showed integrity. In fact, he was regularly in touch with the bank and his creditors, working out a repayment plan.

Tough Questions Make for Clear Thinking

Following our experience in the church in Colorado, we devised a set of questions to help both ourselves and other churches evaluate their financial savvy.

— Do we count and record offerings immediately after they are received? Every moment they sit around uncounted is a moment when they can be dipped in to.

— Are offerings always stored in a secure or well-supervised area?

— Do we count our cash and checks twice for accuracy? To err in addition is human. But the more we check our work, the more we develop careful accounting habits and avoid careless accounting mistakes.

— Do we place offerings in lockbags (money bags provided by the bank requiring a key to open) after counting?

— Do we place the lockbags in a safe or a night depository until the bank opens?

— Do we strictly limit who has access to the safe?

— Do we change the safe combination when someone is no longer authorized to use it?

— Do we make sure that the same person is not involved in more than one of the financial procedures of the church (collecting funds, counting them, recording the giving, authorizing expenditures, writing the checks, auditing the account)? The more access a person has to the various procedures, the greater the ability to misuse funds.

— Are all persons authorized to write checks against church funds held responsible through an accounting/auditing system?

— Do we provide the bank with annual updates of persons authorized to sign checks against *any* account associated with the church? Some banks are, surprisingly, not strict about who signs checks for a church or for a particular program of the church. They know we're a volunteer organization with a high turnover in leadership. We are wise to make sure they know who exactly can write checks, and for what.

— Do we issue annual receipts for giving? This is just another check on determining that what comes in has, in fact, been accounted for.

We found that unless we could give a firm yes to all of these questions, we might have a significant hole in our church financial structure through which we could lose hundreds or perhaps thousands of dollars.

Policies and Procedures Check Personalities

Churches that are not guided by *policies* and *procedures* are vulnerable to being misguided by *personalities*. An opportunist is quick to spot an opportunity.

Good financial policies, however, have multiple benefits: they protect not only the institution but also the individual, not only from temptation but also from accusation.

One problem, of course, is trying to institute new policies with financial people who've been around awhile. They assume policies are changing because others have become suspicious of them.

Sometimes, then, it's best to wait for a changing of the financial guard before instituting policies.

But in any case, it's good to let people know why the changes are taking place.

"If churches simply take appropriate measures to insure that no one is vulnerable, they won't subject their people to possible accusation," an executive pastor told me. "We're not challenging a person's integrity when we develop policies and procedures for handling the church's money. We're just closing the doors so we don't provide the opportunity for misappropriating funds. If we leave the door open for financial abuse, we share the responsibility for what happens."

As I've spoken with other pastors on this issue, I discovered a number of policies common among them:

● *Secure membership in the Evangelical Council for Financial Accountability.* An executive pastor of a large church in Phoenix said this was their first priority in insuring financial integrity. Membership in the ECFA is like receiving the Good Housekeeping Seal of Approval in the area of church finances. This is especially important for larger churches that process huge sums of money on a regular basis.

● *Never allow for presigned checks.* In southeast Asia, a missionary who was a co-signer on the mission's corporate fund had a habit of presigning checks because it was "more convenient." When the bookkeeper filled in one check for several hundred thousand dollars and skipped the country, the missionary went to jail, and the mission was held liable for the bad check.

● *Expenses should be documented.* All requests for reimbursement should come with receipts and be approved by the person responsible for that area of ministry. If for some reason receipts have been lost or were never requested, an individual can at least sign a request for reimbursement that itemizes their expenses.

● *Never pay expenses out of cash offerings.* An executive pastor warns against this practice for two reasons. First, revenues will be understated when the offerings are deposited at the bank, and second, if no receipt is turned in, expense reports will be incorrect.

Even if a receipt is given and the payment duly noted, it makes bookkeeping much more complicated.

- *No checks should ever be written for cash amounts.* Checks written to CASH cannot be justified in an audit. There's simply no way to document where the funds went.

- *Avoid mingling funds.* Monies given for a building fund must be held in reserve for that purpose. If a person designates a gift for something the church doesn't want or need, the funds should be returned to the donor or permission obtained to reassign funds to another area.

One problem with mixing funds is that it's hard to track and pay expenses properly. One ministry organization had the habit of mingling their funds, so that staff support was virtually indistinguishable from operating expenses. As a result, paychecks and reimbursements were often withheld so the organization could cover operating expenses.

- *Do not allow for separate funds.* Separate accounts should not exist in the church's name — at least not without a regular accounting and an annual audit.

For example, a church might think it efficient to open accounts for youth, women's ministries, and the benevolence fund, thinking that it is easier to allow these ministries to process their own funds. The problem, as I personally discovered, is that this can quickly get out of control. Someone needs to be monitoring such accounts on a regular basis to prevent abuse.

- *Secure authorization for use of funds for special purposes.* If the pastor or staff use church funds to help purchase a home, for example, make certain a written agreement is drawn up, and secure official board and/or congregational approval for such a transaction. It should be defined in advance whether those funds are to be repaid upon termination of the pastoral relationship or upon sale of the home.

(A word of caution is in order, however. The church should always consult a tax authority to determine how exactly to set up such funds legally.)

One summer, I visited the offices of an independent church

that had grown rapidly. It was leasing office space and renting a high school auditorium for worship. The church had grown to more than 700 people, had purchased property, and was planning to build.

"What an ideal ministry!" I said to the associate, wishing I were in his place.

When I returned to the Northwest three years later, I discovered that the senior pastor had left under a cloud of suspicion. He had used building funds to buy his home, doing so without adequate board authorization.

A congregation of 700 dwindled overnight to less than 200. I was recently back in the same office with the new pastor, talking with him about ways to rebuild the congregation's credibility.

A Second Opinion Is Needed Annually

For seven years prior to my going to the Colorado church, a perfunctory letter appeared in the church's annual report indicating that all was well with the church's finances. Needless to say, some respected leaders ended up embarrassed when it was disclosed that the church had lost more than $40,000 over eight years.

How did that happen? All those years they had performed an in-house, incomplete, audit.

A church audit is a series of procedures done to (1) test, on a predetermined basis, various financial transactions that occur during the previous year, (2) verify that internal control methods are working, and (3) form an opinion about the appropriateness and clarity of the financial statements presented.

An audit does not, however, guarantee that every transaction was accurately recorded. It is no proof that all funds were handled appropriately.

"An audit is the expression of an opinion," says Manfred Holck, Jr., writing in *The Clergy Journal.* "Through a series of tests and inquiries and probing investigations, the auditor or the auditing committee decides if, based on the information given them, the financial reports do fairly represent the financial condition of the congregation. Based on a testing of selected transactions — checks written and deposits made — and relying on their own experiences, the auditors state as precisely as they can if things seem to be in order."

Pastors I spoke with differed as to whether the audit needed to be done by an outside, independent auditor or handled from within by church members with expertise in financial matters.

At one church in the Northwest, the leadership recently completed an in-house audit. "The important thing," said the pastor, "is that the auditing committee is made up of qualified people who are not associated in any way with the board, the staff, or the finance committee of the church."

In this church, the auditing committee goes through all the books and records each fall. They are entitled to see anything, though they don't look at everything. Every transaction over $1,000 is carefully examined. Transactions under $1,000 are examined on a random basis.

They review the financial process from beginning to end, asking a series of questions that deal with each of the major areas of the church's finances, including cash receipts, cash expenditures, bank statement reconciliation, petty cash funds, individual member contributions, amortization of debt, and securities and investments. At the end of the process, the committee writes a paragraph summary on each area, assessing its strengths and weaknesses, and making recommendations to the church board.

Another executive pastor I spoke with strongly advocates having an outside, independent certified public accountant provide the church with a full audit. And he prefers it be done by a non-Christian, based on his conviction that "the church's finances should look good to all people."

In spite of the expense, he feels it is worth it. Knowing that an annual outside audit will be done gives the staff leverage to insist that certain procedures be followed or documents produced: "Our auditor insists on it." Also, an outside auditor can see more quickly how a budget and financial reports could be confusing and so can recommend appropriate changes. Auditors can quickly get to the heart of matters: they will ask difficult questions because they are not intimidated about offending anyone.

The decision to have an audit done by insiders or by someone from the outside depends to a large degree on the size of a church and the scope of its ministry. The important thing is that it be done thoroughly by qualified individuals who are independent from the church's financial proceedings.

In the end, a dishonest and diligent person can always find a loophole in a church's financial structure, just as a persevering thief can find a way into a secure house. But installing good financial procedures in a church is like installing deadbolts and window jams in a home: it greatly discourages petty thievery, enhances significantly the financial integrity of a church, and protects church workers from accusation.

Part Three
Spending and Investing Money

A church budget is simply someone's priorities for use of church funds. These may or may not be the congregation's priorities, or even the present leadership's, but someone or some group has priorities that determine how money is allocated.

— *Gary Fenton*

CHAPTER TEN

Determining Which Ministry Gets What

"Pastor, we don't have a budget. We just do what the Lord leads us to do."

These words were spoken to me soon after I agreed to be the preacher at a small rural congregation, which used seminary students to fill the pulpit. When the church voted to hire me, they called me "pastor," but I did not function in that capacity. I was at the church only on weekends, and they knew I would probably leave as soon as my seminary days were over.

As an idealistic young student, I liked the thought of having no budget; it created in my mind the picture of a congregation sensitive to the Lord's leadership, without the bureaucracy associated with a budget.

After a few weeks, I mentioned to one of the leading men that I intended to introduce a new ministry in the next church business meeting, which was held at the conclusion of worship. This man asked me several questions about the ministry idea.

Then he said, "Don't bring up your idea this month. Wait at least a month, until I've visited with some of the men of the church. Your idea has merit, but it may not fit in with what some members think."

I found out later that he had called two other men, and they had talked about my idea. They had looked over the church's financial condition and decided I shouldn't broach my idea in the coming business meeting.

I realize now that these three men were not stubborn or unreasonable but practical. My idea wasn't that great, and the church was in more need of other ministries.

What I especially learned, though, was that the church did have a budget! It was in the mind of the three leaders who in conversation determined the financial priorities of the church.

A church budget is simply someone's priorities for use of church funds. These may or may not be the congregation's priorities, or even the present leadership's, but someone or some group has priorities that determine how money is allocated.

Since every church has a budget, we are wise to recognize it and consciously shape it. It may be efficient when a select two or three determine the budget, but it is not healthy.

Of course, once you open up the process to the congregation, even through their elected leaders, you've got to answer the question, "So, how much *should* we give to each ministry and line item?" Answering that question is not always easy, but it is what setting a budget is all about.

Here are some principles I use in helping a church settle that question.

Prepare Yourself

The extent to which the pastor has input in this process depends upon the policy of the church, the tradition of the particular congregation, and the leadership style of the pastor. In order to be effectively involved in the budget process, I found I need to answer the following questions:

• *Who really sets the budget?* Most churches use some type of committee structure to formulate the budget, but a "paper-chase" study of these committees' duties does not usually explain who really determines the budget.

In many churches a budget committee, or a sub-committee of the board, has each church committee and organization turn in their projected costs for the year. The finance committee then evaluates these and puts together a total budget for the church.

In some churches, the finance committee does little more than total the figures turned in and determine how the budget will then be presented to the church. In other churches, the finance committee looks at each committee's or ministry's reports and then evaluates them in terms of church-wide goals and objectives, and, as a result, may alter those figures.

In either case, in most churches, the budget is pretty much set early on by committees or the leaders of those committees. If I want to have input into the budget, I must do it in the right place at the right time.

A pastor friend who moved to a larger church had saved his vision-and-dreams speech for the budget planning meeting of the finance committee. He was frustrated when his ideas had little impact as the committee gathered and tallied figures. It will take another year for his concerns to be reflected in the budget.

He not only needed to begin earlier, he needed to discover who really determined the budget — leaders in each of the committees — and talk with them first.

• *What does the budget reveal about the church's ministry priorities?* I have to understand the actual values of a congregation before I can effectively influence the budget process. And often the budget is the best indication of what the leadership values.

One church I know of has always said that it is a strong missions congregation. A quick glance at the budget seems to confirm this, but a closer look reveals that most items in the mission section of the budget are not really "mission support." It turns out that anything the leadership wanted but thought might be difficult "to sell" to the church was labeled missions.

As a result, the mission section of the budget was bulging with children's and preschool ministry activities. The new minister of education at the church was at first concerned at what appeared to be a lack of funds for her ministry, only to realize that the actual budget priority and her priority were the same.

● *What are the non-negotiables?* Recently, a lay leader in another church asked me for advice. He didn't really want advice, I discovered; he really wanted to complain about his pastor.

A certain bank for a number of years had financed all the church projects. The bank had been good to the church and had waived some fees and never penalized the church for late payments. The bank also had given the church favorable interest rates.

But when interest rates declined, the pastor was recommending that the church refinance at a lower rate with another financial institution. The finance committee voted down the pastor's recommendation. The pastor complained that they were not being good stewards of the Lord's money. The committee felt, by honor, tied to the bank that had seen them through tough times.

Idealistically, a church should be responsive and resilient enough to base all budget expenditures around needs and good stewardship. But churches, because they are people, frequently spend because of feelings, rather than objective reality.

These "sacred cows" do not begin as "golden calves." Generally these non-negotiables were at one time effective means of ministry. But there is not much to be said for fossilized, good ideas and ministries that have outlived their usefulness.

As pastor, I must not only discover quickly these non-negotiables, I want to pay tribute to their contribution to the church. If I'm going to suggest a change, it will have to be after I've gained the respect and trust of the congregation.

And it will have to be a change that is based in respect for the past: "In the past, this system has served us extremely well. I'm thankful for the people who put this practice into effect. For the coming decade, however, we may need a new strategy."

● *Do those who are responsible for building the budgets understand my interpretation of the church's vision?* If the church has a clear and concise mission statement, it makes setting priorities easier, but it does not take away all the difficulties.

Mission statements are subject to interpretation, and often people assume wrongly that because they are on the same page and reading the same words, they have the same pictures on the screen of their minds. But if the leadership does not understand my interpretation of the mission statement, all my attempts to influence the budget will lead to frustration.

One of the casualties of my ministry was a man who in budget committee fought for an issue he thought was important to the staff. He wanted the budget to include a "first class" leadership retreat for the deacons, church officers, and staff. Several factors were weighting the budget committee against this request, including the cost of the retreat and the history of a similar event five years earlier with a different pastor and staff.

This committee member took great risk by arguing for this retreat. After lobbying by phone with the other committee members and eloquently arguing for his position in the meeting, a motion to include the retreat in the budget passed.

The man was soon disappointed when he discovered that none of our staff believed this retreat was essential for the mission of our church.

Looking back, I now realize that when I had visited with him regarding leadership training, I had not fully explained myself. The staff and I believed the church, not the staff, needed a long-term program through which we would identify, develop, and train future leaders. As a result of this misunderstanding, although he did not leave the church, he never again took any significant risks in the committees.

Once the leadership, including me, has a common understanding of where we'd like the church to go, we can begin putting
the dollars-and-cents issues on the table for discussion. All through
the process, though, I aim to understand the views of the lay leadership. For even at the dollars-and-cents stage of budgeting, although
we are now going in the same direction, we sometimes fail to aim at
the same specific target. We may agree that evangelism is our highest priority, for instance, but whether we should invest in evangelism training for members or bring in an evangelist for a week is
another matter.

Avoiding Traps

How we work out disagreements at the dollars-and-cents
stage of finances requires patience, fortitude, and wisdom. Few
people are opposed to a particular line item receiving funding in a
budget, and as a result, the issues often hinge on *the amount* line
items or ministries receive. In the process of determining how
much, congregations can become polarized.

As the discussion ensues, though, the pastor can avoid several traps as the committee or church seeks to determine what
receives how much.

● *The line-item trap.* Someone who places a high priority on
youth ministry notices in the budget that the line item for youth
ministry is only half of that for the music ministry. This person
concludes, with some disappointment and anger, that the church
thinks more of music than youth.

Line items in a budget, however, are usually designed for
administrative purposes. Taken in isolation, they don't necessarily
communicate what a church's feelings are about a ministry. Sometimes you have to dig deeper into the budget to find that out.

In my early months in my present church, a couple of families
met with me regarding the lack of funding for the youth ministry.
Without fully examining the total dollars available to youth ministry, I hastily agreed with them.

I soon found I had spoken too soon. After some research I
discovered that the budget line item for youth ministry shows only

about 40 percent of the funds used in the youth program. But many expenses for youth ministry are scattered throughout the budget, under "administration" and "personnel," for instance. The ministry to youth was more important than the line item showed.

• *The higher-priority-means-more-money trap.* As a pastor and the leadership work through the priorities, they may assume that by giving more money to a ministry they are giving that ministry a higher priority rating. This works on the mistaken assumptions that (a) giving more money is the only way to raise a ministry's status and (b) a church has only one budget.

But every congregation has at least three budgets, and only one is the financial budget. A second and equally important budget is the time budget, which is called the church calendar. To make a ministry a priority may not mean more money but instead involve giving a program a better time slot on the church schedule.

Another budget is the pulpit-emphasis budget. Some priorities, with good time slots and adequate funding, go lacking because they are not emphasized by those who share the pulpit. When properly promoted through the pulpit, though, many ministries can flourish.

Recently, a minister to single adults told me about the turning point in her ministry. A church had called her to build a strong singles ministry. Funding and facilities were provided, but the ministry did not really have the support of the church until the pastor wrote a column in the church newsletter regarding the singles ministry and asked two single people to lead in prayer during worship.

This young minister said that the senior pastor's public endorsement was more valuable than a large increase in funds.

• *The easy-compromise trap.* Budget preparation time is one of the most stressful times of the year. Competing priorities bring inevitable conflict. In churches with large staffs these conflicts can escalate into ego wars, with staff members becoming battalion commanders and members, the ground troops.

The pastor may try to avoid these conflicts and quickly seek compromises: The missions people and the youth ministry people each want 10 percent increases for their respective ministries, but there is only enough money to give 10 percent to one. Solution? Of course, give 5 percent increases to each.

Often, however, these compromises, although they reduce tension, fail to construct a budget according to the church's priorities. If the church has previously determined that youth ministry was to be the top priority for the coming five years, then the compromise has done the church a disservice.

Certainly compromise is necessary in every budget process, but if everything falls into place without healthy confrontation and discussion of church priorities, it may mean that the official priorities of the church have been put aside for the comfort of church leaders.

• *The meaningless-motto trap.* One temptation is to have the church's priorities articulated in words and mottoes that have no relationship to reality.

Last year I received a copy of a church budget that had BAL-ANCED MINISTRY printed across the top of the page. The budget was divided into four areas: evangelism, missions, ministry, and worship. Line items were listed under each area. Each of the areas equaled one-fourth of the budget. It was obvious, though, that someone had spent time adjusting figures and tinkering with the process so that they would be equal.

Although every church does have to seek balance, it is wrong to assume that balance must be measured in terms of equal funding.

Guidelines for Effective Change

The church has difficulty changing because its message appears to contradict the call to change. The message of Christ is the same yesterday, today, and forever, but the careless member may hear that the *church* is the same yesterday, today, and forever.

The church budget, since it reflects ministry with people, has to be dynamic. It will have to change significantly from time to time. I've never found that pressure, political power, and smooth pulpit rhetoric encourage change as effectively as education, pastoral care — and patience.

In particular, in seeking to help a church make significant

changes in a budget, I've found the following guidelines helpful.

● *Be prepared for passionate resistance.* Any change brings resistance, but change regarding the use of money brings resistance with passion.

People and organizations are dealing with values when they spend money. How we spend our money says a lot (although not everything) about what we believe is important.

At the same time, the church attracts people to whom values are important, and it continues to teach them that values are important.

Consequently, when values-driven people are encouraged to change how they spend their money, there will be sparks. The old line, "Let's not fight over money," doesn't work in the church precisely because we know that money represents something more than dollars.

The pastor, therefore, should not see all resistance as evil. We best encourage change when we allow people to disagree without questioning their virtue or spirituality.

● *Introduce the change before you request the change.* We pastors often see ourselves as the only one with real vision, and we act as if laypeople never have the courage to do what the Lord wants. I have found, however, that not only are laypeople as courageous as clergy but also that I am less visionary than I sometimes think.

Sometime ago I was in a meeting concerning charitable giving, and one of the speakers discussed the trend toward designated, or donor-directed, giving. I found myself resisting this idea, as I had been a strong advocate of unified-budget giving.

It took about six weeks and a couple of articles in a periodical for me to see the virtues and the possibilities of designated giving. When I did see its value, I discussed it with our finance chairman.

He was opposed to the idea for the very reasons I had been. It became obvious that the idea was not ready to be discussed with the entire committee.

I noticed, though, that I was angry that the chairman, as well as the committee, did not immediately share my enthusiasm! When

I remembered my journey, I was able to be a little more patient.

● *Go slow with changes in philosophy.* Almost any church can be maneuvered or manipulated into making temporary changes in the funding process. Most members can be persuaded to postpone or delay their favorite ministry projects if they believe these projects will soon be restored to their previous levels of funding.

But some changes are not intended to be temporary but indicate a major philosophy shift. To deliberately minimize philosophical changes is not only dishonest, it is shortsighted. Individuals and constituency who have accepted a "temporary" change in the budget process only to find out it is permanent feel violated.

A good rule of thumb: The longer the impact of a change, the slower the change should be paced.

One of my predecessors changed the deacons from being an administrative board (making decisions for the church) to a ministry group (concerned with meeting people's needs). This change, though, removed the deacons from the budget process and permitted women to serve as deacons.

Such a fundamental change, however, didn't happen overnight. This wise pastor led the church to this position over a number of years, and the pace was slow. Now eighteen years later, this deacon ministry is alive and well.

● *Let people know where you're going.* People who know where they're going are best prepared for intersections and curves on the roadway. Likewise, ease in budgeting is directly related to a clear vision of the destination, and that means a clearly defined mission statement.

I am becoming increasingly impressed with the practical value of a congregation having a church vision, or mission statement. By encouraging the church to participate in formulating the mission statement, the pastor not only builds stronger statements but also gives the members ownership of the church's direction. Then when the pastor addresses the vision from the pulpit, he or she is not seen as a modern Moses chiding people for their failure but as a leader who is holding before them a map showing where together they are going.

I've found that I need to articulate the church vision in a sermon at least once a quarter. In fact, one Sunday each year we call "Vision Sunday," at which I preach about the church's vision. We push for attendance and pull out the "bells and whistles." But at least three other times during the year, I preach on the vision, without labeling it as such, trying to find different ways to express the same theme as on Vision Sunday.

• *Listen for underlying issues.* Budget battles may not be about money but about someone's personal crisis. The opposition may not result so much from differing priorities as from a hurt or misunderstanding. Often conflicts over a change in budgeting provide an opportunity to find the real issue.

An individual in a church I previously served was highly vocal about a change the budget committee was proposing. This man had used his Sunday morning Bible study class as a platform to oppose the new budget.

When I heard one Sunday afternoon of his abuse of his role as teacher, I was angry and ready to confront him, but his wife called me before I had the chance. She suggested I go by and see him at work, saying, "He really needs his pastor right now."

When I went by his office on the following Monday, he told me of the discouragement he felt about his work and how a remark I had made in the pulpit appeared to be insensitive to people in his situation. At the conclusion of the visit, he told me he owed me an apology for what he had done in the previous day's Bible study hour.

Later one of our older, wiser church leaders explained to me, "Pastor, it's not socially acceptable to stand in a Bible study class and oppose your pastor for his insensitivity, but it is acceptable to oppose the programs your pastor supports."

• *Maintain your character even if you have to modify your vision.* Vision and mission are changeable. Character is a non-negotiable. Leading a church to redirect its resources will be an ongoing process for the pastor, requiring compromise and a change in direction from time to time. But rarely do you lose your ministry in a local congregation over a disagreement regarding funding.

Sometimes, though, in an uncompromising passion to sell our vision to the congregation, we modify our character. The results are usually disastrous.

A highly respected pastor in one community I served wanted his church to have their own retreat center. He was a visionary leader who could inspire people to follow him. But in the process of selling this idea, he exaggerated the benefits offered by one of the proposed sites, and he publicly lost his temper with one family who questioned him in the process.

The church voted to buy the retreat center, but from then on, the church discussed less his visionary ideas and more his character. He eventually left the church, bitter and angry, even though for several years he had been highly effective.

Our vision can be modified more easily than our character repaired and restored.

Determining which gets how much challenges churches regularly. And helping a church change the level of funding for items is a bigger challenge still. *Challenge*, of course, puts it mildly.

Still, all of this work — and often it is just that — comes down to helping our congregations accomplish their calling. And helping a church do that, no matter the challenge, is central to our ministry.

In terms of spending, the more control the board exerts, the less a ministry can respond immediately to current needs. The more freedom ministries have, the harder it is for the board to monitor exactly what's going on. Each church has to find the middle ground.

— *Richard L. Bergstrom*

CHAPTER ELEVEN

Who Spends the Church's Money?

Each month the trustees faithfully gathered to pay the bills of Community Church. Each month they were greeted by the familiar stack of invoices and requests for reimbursements from church members. And each month they were faced with the same types of questions:

— Which ministry is this new tape recorder to be charged against?

— Who charged $139.50 at the Christian bookstore? Are these books for Sunday school or youth ministry?

— What was the $48.79 worth of groceries charged at Safeway used for?

— Where is the receipt for the supplies purchased for women's ministry?

— There's no budget for computer software; why did the secretary purchase this without prior approval?

— The copy machine expense is running at three times the budget. How are we supposed to pay for this?

An annual budget had been carefully worked out by the staff and the board and approved by the congregation — still, the trustees didn't seem to be able to monitor spending. They couldn't really tell how much each ministry was costing the church.

From time to time, someone suggested they use a purchase-order system, requiring each person making a purchase on behalf of the church to get approval. Unfortunately, that policy also happens to be effective at hindering ministry, making simple purchases time consuming and awkward.

For instance, Bob works as a sponsor for the junior high ministry. He wants to buy some prizes for the upcoming overnight. In Bob's church, everyone is required to have expenditures approved by the church treasurer prior to purchase.

Unfortunately, Bob works long hours in construction and can't get by the church to get a purchase order issued and signed before the event. He decides to turn in the receipt after the fact — and anticipates receiving a lecture from the church treasurer.

Every church has to find a way to avoid cumbersome reporting of purchases and yet accurately monitor expenses. Depending on a church's denomination and traditions, the solutions will look different. Still, here is how many churches have effectively accomplished both of these goals.

Develop the Budget Around Ministry Categories

After our financial crisis in the Colorado church, we decided to rearrange the budget according to ministry categories. Previously the trustees had arranged the budget around categories that made sense to them.

For example, the budget report listed major headings such as SALARIES, UTILITIES, SUPPLIES, YOUTH, EVANGELISM, CHILDREN'S CHURCH, MAINTENANCE, SUNDAY SCHOOL, and OTHER.

The problem with this system, we found, was that it was difficult to attach responsibility to any one individual for a specific category of ministry, as we wanted.

So we changed the report so that all of the budget items relating to a ministry area were brought together.

For instance, in Christian education, everything that was spent for CE, including such items as postage for returning videos, literature for Sunday school, and puppets for children's church — items that were formerly scattered throughout the budget under POSTAGE, SUPPLIES, and CHILDREN'S CHURCH — were placed as line items under the CE budget.

This helped us see clearly how much exactly each ministry was costing us.

After the change, we also saw that church leaders felt more responsible for church finances: they knew what their ministry's financial parameters were and tried to stay within their budgets. This system, of course, had its own drawbacks. For instance, we found that it required a good deal more research and time to document where the money was being spent and which account to charge it against.

But in order to get the advantage of tracking expenses accurately, we felt it was worth the trouble.

Give Individuals Responsibility for an Area of Ministry

I worked with a church in the Northwest that went through a major restructuring of its ministry. Part of the problem in its past had been a fuzziness about the *levels* of responsibility and authority.

For example, if the youth leader wanted to spend money on an outreach activity, he felt he would have to clear it first with the pastor. If the leader of the women's ministry wanted to order Bible study materials, she might first call the church office. That put the pastoral staff, even the church secretary, in the position of approving each request. It was cumbersome, to say the least.

So I helped the church design a new structure, in which levels of responsibility and authority were delineated. In each program area, we gave the leaders (called "the program team") responsibility for both programming and budget within their area of ministry. They were also part of a larger "ministry team," which was overseen by a member of the governing board of the church.

For example, the youth ministry team was composed of the junior high program team, the senior high program team, and the college/career program team.

Thus it became easier to manage the financial affairs of the ministry. Lay leaders were involved more in the budgeting process. They would now come together with staff to prepare their program's budget based on program goals and objectives upon which staff and lay leaders together had previously agreed.

And once the budget was established, the ministry teams were charged with the oversight of their budget, with one person in particular responsible for monitoring finances.

The youth director, for example, was given responsibility for the youth budget. So, if the senior high Bible study leader wanted materials for a discipleship group, he came to the youth director to see where it would come out of the budget.

In the same way, the office administrator didn't have to ask permission of the board every time she needed to order a ream of paper or repairs on the copy machine. She simply looked at her budget, established the line item account number assigned to that, and ordered the material she needed.

But what if a ministry team wishes to change their priorities midway through the fiscal year? Suppose, for instance, that instead of spending $250 on film rental, the youth ministry team thought, because of input from the new youth officers, it should spend $250 on a week-long bike trek — a completely unbudgeted item. Should they be entitled to make that decision on their own? What other factors besides finances might need to be considered in this change of plans? The church board, for example, might have questions about safety and liability that go beyond the budget itself.

One executive pastor I spoke with warned that a board loses its authority to monitor ministry activities if it stops requiring ministries to report changes in their spending plans. Budget approval implies approval of the activities for which those monies are allocated.

Other pastors feel that as long as a ministry sticks to the overall bottom line figure of their ministry, they should have the freedom to make any changes they want.

It depends, then, on how much freedom ministries should be given and how much control the board wants. The more control, the less a ministry can respond immediately to current needs. The more freedom ministries have, the harder it is for the board to monitor exactly what's going on. Each church has to find the middle ground.

Appoint One Person to Monitor the Budget

Even though department heads might monitor the individual purchases, someone still needs to keep an eye on the entire budget, holding the department heads accountable for their choices.

Dick Stunden serves as the church administrator at Bethany Bible Church in Phoenix. As such, he is responsible for monitoring the church budget. The buck stops (literally) on his desk.

He works with each department of the church to develop a detailed annual budget. If a staff member spends more in his or her budget area, Stunden is the one to bring it to the department head's attention. If an unauthorized expenditure shows up for payment, Stunden will put a tracer on it to find out who spent it and where it is to be paid for out of the budget.

"The idea," he says, "is to find the balance between trust and accountability." Stunden's intent is not to exert undue control over expenditures. The budget, he explains, is a tool to hold everyone accountable. But the budget cannot foresee all problems. "I won't complain about an overage in one area of a department's budget," he says, "as long as they adhere to their bottom line."

One administrative pastor told me, "We have a CPA who

actually writes the checks, and then I countersign them. Since we both oversee the whole budget, we can see right away if the request is inappropriate or out of line. We can catch it at that point."

The person monitoring the budget and/or the person signing the checks, however, shouldn't necessarily have veto power over check requests. That's better left in the hands of the individual program team leaders.

In particular, one veteran pastor notes, "The one person monitoring the budget should not be the church treasurer. The treasurer's job is to release funds as approved by the church budget and designated by the staff or layperson in charge. All too often, well-intended treasurers become uninvited watchdogs of church funds."

I was visiting with a pastor recently in his study when in walked an elderly woman, who proceeded to open his desk drawer in search for some keys.

He turned to me and said, "Dick, I'd like you to meet Gladys, our church secretary. She's also the church treasurer."

"Yes," replied Gladys. "I've been doing both jobs for thirty years."

After she left, I asked the pastor, "It sounds as if Gladys may have a lot of control over the church's finances."

"It is difficult to get anything approved without Gladys's approval," he conceded. "But she's been our most faithful worker in the church."

"I'm sure she has been," I replied. "But how do you wrest control of the church's purse strings from someone like that?"

"I don't know, other than to wait for her to retire," the pastor replied. "Fortunately, she is doing just that at the end of this year. Then I'll institute some defined policies that will make it more difficult for one person to obtain veto power over expenses."

Require Advanced Approval of Non-Budgeted Items

The annual budget cannot predict every expense that will be incurred throughout the course of the year. Plans change, opportunities arise, and emergencies occur unexpectedly:

— The college department decides to bring in a nationally known speaker for their spring break. The change in plans adds $500 to the cost of the event.

— The pastor decides he wants to go to a pastors' conference 900 miles away. His additional travel and expense is $1,000 more than budget allows for the conference.

— An exceptionally heavy winter snow adds $1,500 to the cost of snow removal from the parking lot.

— The breakdown of the copy machine requires an unbudgeted expense of $5,000 to replace it.

All of these are either unbudgeted items or represent expenses in excess of projections. Although each expense at the time may seem utterly reasonable, it is wise to get official approval before spending the money. What seems like a "clear need" or "an opportunity not to be missed" to one person or group may seem like a mere luxury to another. The safe assumption is this: If it's not in the budget, the jury is out as to whether it's a justifiable expense.

A church in a community where I once served ended up in foreclosure. A public auction for the church's property and buildings was scheduled for a Saturday morning at ten o'clock. How did it get to that point?

The church never had an opportunity to decide on expenses incurred beyond the budget. The pastor had a free hand in obligating the church for the many extra expenses that occurred during the building program. He thought, *Well, we've got to have the building, so I guess we have no choice.*

If he had taken some counsel, a few more choices might have occurred to him. As it was, when the building was finally completed, a congregation of eight-five giving units was indebted over a million dollars.

Fortunately, the denomination bought up the notes and saved the ministry of the church — but not before requiring the pastor to step down and leave town!

In addition, once permission to spend beyond budget is received, rather than changing the budget figures to reflect the overages, most churches find it best to leave the original budget figures in place. That way, when it comes time to plan the next year's budget, the finance committee can look at the original budget and compare it with normal costs, not the emergency costs.

Try to Reimburse People for Ministry Expenses

One of the hardest ministry expenses to track are those incurred by people who refuse to turn in their receipts to get reimbursed. They feel this is one way they can contribute to the church; besides, they feel it may be petty to ask for reimbursement every time they spend two or three dollars for the church.

Those two or three dollars, however, multiplied by many people and many occasions add up. And that makes for a number of problems:

— It makes it impossible to figure out how much it actually costs to run a ministry.

— It puts unfair pressure on those who follow in that ministry to do the same. That may make recruitment more difficult.

— It takes the control out of the church's hands for determining its financial priorities.

— The person spending the money may lose out on a tax deduction (if they itemize deductions). The church has no way of confirming their gifts.

I have mixed feelings, though, about such a practice. On the one hand, if a church is to track where its monies are being spent, it needs to develop a comprehensive church budget that includes these hidden costs that people cover out of their own pockets.

On the other hand, reimbursement procedures for some churches are cumbersome — it's too much trouble for small expenses. In addition, I don't know that a church really wants to take away people's spontaneous generosity.

Churches in this situation may have to accept the practice, and therefore, assume its liabilities. In small churches, this may be an ingrained habit that simply can't be broken anyway. It wouldn't be worth it politically to try!

Or churches can ease reimbursement procedures, allowing people to estimate their expenses and turn in many at once. This saves people the trouble of saving small receipts and turning them in one by one. This generally works, however, for reimbursing only minor expenditures, for coffee, small stationary supplies, and the like.

Eliminate Charge Accounts That Can't Provide Receipts

In one church I served, we used a church charge account at a grocery store. That proved to be an unreliable means of documenting charges and thus recording how exactly our money was being spent.

Each month groceries showed up charged against the church's account. We couldn't tell, however, who charged what. The invoice indicated only the date and amount of the transaction. It was impossible to discern whether the items charged went to the youth program, the women's ministry, the fellowship committee, or someone's personal groceries. Some people would turn in their receipts faithfully, but others never did get into the habit.

This, apparently, is not an unusual problem. I recently spoke with a church administrator from another church facing a similar situation. He confirmed the dilemma: "And the pastor is the biggest culprit!" he told me. "He never remembers to turn in his receipts from the Christian bookstore."

In my church, we notified the grocery store that we needed a more specific accounting of what was being charged in the name of the church. When they told us they couldn't do that, we decided to close the charge account.

An alternative to charge accounts is to beef up the petty-cash fund. For many churches, issuing advances and requiring receipts seems to be a much better way to monitor their expenses.

Again the tension is felt, though. In a large church, this can become cumbersome, unless each department has its own petty-cash fund.

Just Say No!

If the budget is experiencing a shortfall, several key questions need to be asked:

— Is this month's downturn typical? If so, the problem may safely be ignored for a month or two. If not, it's time to pay attention.

— Are income and expenses where they should be according to our projections? If not, why not?

— And if not, were the extra expenses approved? If not, the hole in the system must be plugged at once.

— If approved and over budget, what are we going to do about it? Have a special appeal or cut spending?

Sometimes, of course, a special appeal is out of order. A time comes in the life of many churches when slowing spending is necessary. There is no pleasant way of doing this, of course, but some ways make more sense.

When one church I served faced just such a shortfall, the finance committee went through the budget, item by item, marking each item with a red, yellow, or green highlighter.

Green items were to remain in the budget as scheduled: the utility bill, the mortgage, insurance payments, and staff salaries.

Yellow items meant exercise caution and spend only as needed: Sunday school materials, janitorial supplies, and advertising.

Red items were put on hold until the financial situation improved: staff conferences, continuing education, subsidies for lay training, capital expenditures, film rentals for youth programs.

All staff and lay leaders were then notified of the status of their accounts.

In difficult times, everyone must be willing to tighten their belts, and that often includes the pastor. And sometimes it's the example of the pastor that can help a church turn a corner.

A pastor in the Northwest confided in me that the quickest way to alert the congregation to the financial shortfall was for him to go to work part-time in construction. It was amazing, he told me, to see how quickly the shortfall was reversed once his parishioners observed him working away from the church office to make ends meet!

Every church needs to be concerned about who spends the church's money and how exactly it is spent. That's what good stewardship is about. We may not have to require every individual making a purchase to fill out a purchase order for every purchase. But by wisely delegating authority, we practice good stewardship, and ministry can keep moving forward.

Churches often fail to count the hidden costs of poor salaries.

— Wayne Pohl

CHAPTER TWELVE

Setting Staff Salaries

The importance of paying pastors an adequate wage was a lesson learned the hard way early in my ministry.

I graduated near the top of my seminary class. I had high hopes of securing a well-paying position, yet my first call was to a mission congregation. To my knowledge, I was offered the lowest salary of anyone in my graduating class. Of course, I accepted the call, failing to realize the impact an inadequate income could have on the morale of me and my family. To use a biblical phrase, I was zealous without knowledge.

Trying to set an example for my flock, I even tithed on this substandard salary.

One Saturday my wife and I were out canvassing the neighborhood on behalf of the church. About noon we decided to stop at Burger King and grab lunch. We were tired and hungry as we stepped up to the counter. After we ordered, we each looked to the other to pay. As we opened our wallets, we realized that neither of us had enough money to pay for our burgers. We left in embarrassment. My wife is a naturally up person and rarely cries. That day she wept.

Unfortunately, similar scenarios occur in churches around the country. Pastors in far too many places are underpaid. Churches often fail to count the hidden costs of poor salaries. Individuals do not work effectively when money is a constant worry. They become resentful, unproductive, and the ministry suffers. Their families bear the scars for years to come.

Now that I'm in a different position, in which I have a bit more influence over my own salary and those of our staff, my philosophy is that pastors should be free from money worries, as much as possible, so they can concentrate on ministry.

We don't want to overpay or underpay. We don't want anyone to stay at our church only because they couldn't get the same salary elsewhere. Likewise, we don't want anyone to leave solely on account of money. We seek to remove money as a preoccupation.

Our goal is to keep productive and hard-working staff free from humiliating circumstances such as those my wife and I experienced early on in our ministry. Not incidentally, our staff turnover rate has been small through the years.

A Difficult Question

This is not to say that arriving at a proper wage for a pastor or staff member is always an easy process. In times of economic downturn or recession, the problem can become even more difficult.

Back in the early 1980s, our city was hit hard by a recession and layoffs. Because our city is so closely tied to the automobile industry, the sluggish economy had resulted in a 20 to 25 percent unemployment rate.

One Tuesday evening during this recession, our elder board met to determine proposed raises for staff for the coming year. Several families in our church were unemployed. We even began a support group for jobless men who had nowhere to go in the morning. The irony was, despite the bad economic news on the outside, our church was doing well financially. We had seen growth both in membership and giving.

That evening I watched as our elder board agonized over a pay increase. They struggled to reconcile the grim conditions of the city's economy with the legitimate needs of the pastoral staff. A large pay increase might convey insensitivity to those in the congregation who were in difficult straits. A minimal increase might discourage the staff who had worked hard and productively that year. Arguments on both sides of the issue were convincing. Eventually the elders compromised, and the staff received a modest increase, somewhat less than what we would have received under normal conditions.

The next morning the first knock on my office door was from an elder. Don sat down and calmly informed me he was resigning from the elder board. He simply could not live with the pay increase enacted the night before. He felt it was excessive, given the hardship many in the congregation were facing and in light of the city's hard times. I asked him to avoid making a rash decision and to pray about the matter for a week or so.

That afternoon another elder knocked on my office door. He too had come with a purpose in mind. John didn't feel it was right to catch me by surprise, so he had come in person to explain why he was leaving the elder board. He couldn't live with the pittance of a raise the elder board had voted for the staff. John felt it was unjust, regardless of the economy, to penalize the staff after such an outstanding year at the church. I asked him to wait on his decision, to pray about it for a week, and then call me again.

Fortunately, both men relented of their decisions to resign. But the situation illustrates how difficult it is to arrive at staff salaries that everyone can feel good about. The issue of compensation can become emotionally charged and highly volatile if not handled in an orderly fashion.

Who Should Get Paid?

A basic question needs to be answered in discussing staff salaries: Who should be paid and who should not? The church is heavily dependent on volunteers. The list of people who normally work without financial compensation is long in most churches. Teachers, ushers, kitchen workers, music personnel, and a host of other positions are often staffed by volunteers. No one, including most church boards, wants to pay for something you can get for free.

But there are situations where a volunteer simply won't do. When should you begin to pay someone for their ministry to the church? We follow two guidelines:

First, we determine the level of expertise needed to do the job. I went from a small mission congregation to a congregation of 2,000 people. I discovered there was a great difference in the time and ability needed to manage a Sunday school of 50 children versus 500 students. As the complexity of the situation grows, so does the need for a paid staff member.

Second, we ask if the quality of the program will diminish without a paid staff position. We operate a vacation Bible school in the summer on three separate campuses. A program of that size takes exceptional management skills simply to handle logistical matters. Coordinating volunteers, transportation, and curriculum for a large vbs demands attention to maintain quality. If a paid staff member was not overseeing our operation on these three campuses, the ministry would collapse under its own weight.

That, however, is the beauty of moving volunteers into staff positions. As ministries grow, our staff grows. We enjoy hiring from within the congregation. It's been wonderful to watch qualified lay people be trained for ministry and then join our staff.

There are several advantages to growing your own team. They blend well with the existing staff; they understand the ministry; and they are trusted by the congregation. By promoting from within we often save up to seven years in the time needed to make someone truly effective.

The Right Staff Members Pay for Themselves

We try to pay individuals based on their contribution to the ministry. Performance and results play a big part in this decision.

In setting an initial salary, the elder board determines a top and bottom cost barrier. Once that's established, we look at the individual's position, experience, and education. Their ministry record plays a part in our decision making. Someone who produced elsewhere is likely to produce in our setting as well. We look for achievers. Why? Because they tend to achieve. It's much easier to set salaries for producers than it is for those who seem to retire on the job. The producers eventually pay for themselves, and then some.

For example, we discovered that the single largest demographic group in our congregation was the 15- to 19-year-old age group. Yet, we had to admit honestly we were doing little to minister to these teenagers.

Then we hired a young man as youth pastor who I believed was a winner from day one. Our youth program boomed. His high school choir programs attracted parents and other relatives. Unchurched families began to seek out the church to see what it offered their children. He turned inactive families with teenagers into active participants in the life of the church. While the primary goal of all this was ministry to kids and their families, it resulted in increased financial giving. The enthusiasm he generated for the church eventually reached people's wallets.

It is a fair and valid question to ask, "What is an individual worth to our congregation?" I believe that the right person will pay for himself or herself within two years. That goes for other positions besides youth pastor.

When our music minister came to the church, we had fifty people involved in the music ministry. Within two years, 250 people were active. He developed a concert series that drew patron dollars. He began a music academy at the church. He saw his job as more than playing the organ; his job was to build a ministry. As a result, financially we gained far more than we spent on his salary.

At the same time, hiring the wrong individuals can cost a great deal. A secretary with poor phone skills can quickly sour the image of the church. A custodian who resents the wear and tear on the church and continually reprimands members is costing some congregations money. Any individual who adversely affects the ministry of the church will eventually be a drain financially to the congregation.

The Mean Doesn't Always Work

Some have suggested that the senior pastor ought to make the equivalent of the average income of the entire congregation. In principle the idea is misguided, yet in practice, many churches follow this maxim. The reason is simple: Whether we admit it or not, all of us evaluate what others should make based on what we make. Whoever sets a pastor's salary cannot help but compare their own earnings with his. But is this always fair?

Let's say the average household income in a congregation is $40,000. Let's say the average wage earner manages a retail outlet, has five years' experience, and a bachelor's degree. The store has shown a profit some years, a loss others.

Now let's say the pastor has two bachelor's degrees and two master's degrees — as much education as any lawyer in his congregation. He's been at this job for twenty-five years, the congregation has grown by 300 percent, and the budget has grown tenfold. He manages a staff of six individuals and in addition puts in long hours dealing with highly stressful situations.

Now, should this pastor be paid exactly the same as the retail manager who has limited experience, a lesser education, and mixed sales results? That would be unfair. Such policies not only discourage capable pastors but push capable pastors to seek churches elsewhere.

What happens when the average income of a congregation is much higher than the senior pastor's wages? Perhaps it should not be this way, but all of us assign a measure of respect to individuals according to what they earn. For example, college basketball coaches have turned down professional NBA positions because their players would be making two or three times their salary. Who is going to listen to whom under those circumstances?

The same principle applies to the church. Affluent parishioners will have a difficult time respecting the pastor when he is making less than half of their income. In that setting, leadership will be a difficult task.

Is Every Angel Worth the Same?

I bristle at the notion that all staff members should be paid the same. This makes no more sense than the idea that the pastor should make the average mean salary of the congregation.

It could be called the "littlest angel theory." It goes something like this: Every individual, though each might differ in gifts and abilities, is of equal value to the church. Therefore everyone should be paid the same to avoid showing partiality, a sin which Scripture condemns.

This is a distortion of biblical thinking and sound business practice. It completely sets aside the teaching on diligence, rewards for investment of talents, and the idea of fairness.

Should an effective music minister whose program is booming and reaching hundreds in the community be paid the same as an individual who plods along, perhaps alienating more individuals than he attracts? Sooner or later the person making the extraordinary effort will ask, "Why am I working so hard when others, who do far less, get the same reward as I do?" People need to be rewarded for effort, and a positive evaluation coupled with a monetary reward is a strong motivational tool.

The idea that everyone should make the same salary as the next person is irrational. Should I pay someone simply for breathing? Such forced equality is the ultimate unfairness.

Playing to Great Reviews

The actual process of establishing salary increases for the

coming year begins in the staff care committee. That committee meets with representatives from the finance committee to determine what range of increases we can afford for the next fiscal year. Last year we settled in the range of 2.9 percent minimum to 8 percent maximum. There's no use in promising staff members raises that the congregation can't deliver. So to be realistic, we have to first determine what the giving potential is for the next year.

Our minimum figure is never less than the annual cost-of-living index. We have been able to keep pace with that for all but two of the seventeen years I've been pastor here. There were two years in the late 1970s when inflation was running in excess of 14 percent a year. We simply could not afford those increases.

When the staff care committee has determined the range of salary increases for the year, the elder chairman, acting as their representative, brings the recommendations to me. It is then my job to evaluate each of the staff members who report directly to me. In turn, each staff member who supervises employees is charged with evaluating their work.

We are results oriented in our philosophy. In evaluating, we see if their program has resulted in growth and expansion. Have they gone beyond maintenance to achieving significant goals that have benefited the entire church?

Rather than have a department evaluate an individual, I'll let the statistics do the talking. I'll examine what percentage increase that department experienced that year. That's an evaluation you can work with. If demographic changes in our community make growth difficult or impossible, I take that into account. This is also an excellent time to review a person's strengths and weaknesses.

I'll often take my employees out to lunch one by one. I will have a salary-increase figure in mind. If it is different from what they feel is justified, I'll allow them to make their case. Occasionally I'll change my mind, but usually I stay close to the figure I've established.

We recognize that people on our staff respond differently to a self-evaluation. So we try and tailor the evaluation to people's personalities. If they are more technically oriented, we have them fill out a more objective evaluation. If they are more verbal, we allow them to write extended answers.

It's important to remember that when you are establishing the salary level of another individual, they are a brother or sister in the Lord. However, that should motivate us to be more open and candid in our evaluations rather than less. We owe it to them to tell the truth in a candid but gracious manner.

We conduct our evaluations in May and June even though the actual budget process does not begin until the fall. The reasons are simple. The peak of any program in a given church year is reached in May. It would be grossly unfair to evaluate a program in the dog days of August, when many parishioners have dropped out of sight or headed for their lake cabins. It's much easier to do a statistical examination of a program in the late spring rather than late summer. Results are more on the minds of everyone as the programs come to an end.

I'm evaluated by the chairman of the board of elders. I have long believed that it's virtually impossible to be evaluated coherently by a board. It is guaranteed schizophrenia. On any given board you'll have members who admire and love you, and others that would love to see you leave at the earliest possible moment. So the chairman filters all the input and presents my performance review in a coherent way.

We can take a lesson from the business world. As much as possible, individuals do not report to boards, but to other individuals. I recognize the risks involved in giving so much authority to one person in the evaluation process, but I would rather be evaluated by one person than by a group, especially a group that is changing every year.

Of course, simply because a supervisor recommends a particular salary doesn't mean it is automatically granted. All such recommendations are taken back to the elder board for their final approval. They force us to justify the recommended salary increases to insure fairness.

Once we are agreed on the figures, however, it allows us to present a united front in presenting them to the congregation. When someone asks how we arrived at these income figures, we reply that it was the decision of the pastor, the chairman of the elders, and a special committee of elders that proposed them. That helps to distribute the responsibility.

For Our Eyes Only

I'm a firm believer in keeping salaries confidential. That's why we lump the salaries in three categories in the budget. When they are presented to the annual meeting, we list one budget for senior administrators, one for coordinators, and one for administrative assistants. It is very unusual for one staff member to discover what another is making.

It does happen occasionally, however. I had a secretary quit one year because she discovered a co-worker was making a nickel an hour more than she was. She resigned in protest, and I was more than willing to accept such a resignation. We don't need that kind of attitude in our work place.

Though in some denominations the staff salaries are a matter of public record, I believe such a practice is demoralizing. It would embarrass some of my staff for the congregation to know what they were making. They are not particularly great performers at this point, and their salaries reflect that judgment. Those receiving higher salaries should not have to justify that to the congregation or other members of the staff. I believe it is better to keep such matters confidential.

Policies to Promote Loyalty

I sincerely desire long tenures for my staff members. We've had an education person with us for ten years. Our administrative secretary has been here for thirteen years. Most of our staff have been here more than a decade, which is rare in churches today.

When we lose someone of high quality, it has actually tended to help our salaries. The elder board realizes that they had better pay us according to our worth or another church will do so. When an associate went to Iowa for an $18,000 increase, the message was not lost on our board.

We also try to create an environment that is caring and

compassionate for employees. When a secretary has a son at home with a 105-degree fever, we release her from her work without penalty. We know that her mind is at home, and that's where she belongs that day.

When our staff receive offers to perform weddings or take special speaking engagements, we don't ask for the honorarium. They are the ones who earn it, and they should keep it. However, simply because they are called to minister elsewhere for a week does not negate the work they are expected to have completed here. Such outside obligations are understood as time above and beyond their normal work load. If they can handle the time away and still complete their tasks, we encourage them to take advantage of the opportunity.

The point of all this, of course, is the original premise: we want to free individuals from money worries so they give their best to their ministry. We want no one to stay or leave on account of salary.

The day my wife and I left Burger King hungry and penniless, I realized that the issue of just compensation for those in the ministry is an issue no pastor or church can afford to avoid.

Unlike the subjective and internal aspects of Christianity,
money is like a hanging string, weighted at the end with
iron, pulled straight by gravity — it indicates precisely
what is vertical or slanted; it objectively measures our lives.
— Craig Brian Larson

Epilogue

Weighty words have anchored these chapters. *Integrity. Trust-worthiness. Responsibility. Faith. Wisdom. Leadership.* When discussing church finances, that spirit of *gravitas*, of probity, of importance, is well suited, for money is a kingdom plumb line.

Unlike the subjective and internal aspects of Christianity, money is like a hanging string, weighted at the end with iron, pulled straight by gravity — it indicates precisely what is vertical or slanted; it objectively measures our lives.

Observing how a pastor manages money, God can plumb the

mysteries of the heart and discover spiritual values, heavenly priorities, faithfulness, honesty, love, commitment. Or the dark opposite. Jesus entrusted the alms bag to Judas. A coincidence? Judas pilfered the bag. Shortly thereafter, he remained hellishly in character when he pecked Christ with the kiss of betrayal and death.

If leaders cherish integrity, they will attend to the income and expenses. If they want to prove themselves capable of shouldering increased responsibility, they will keep an honest eye on the budget.

Circumstances differ, so not every pastor will attend to finances to the same extent. But even given our differences, is it going too far to say, seek ye first to be faithful with finances, and the kingdom shall be added unto you as well?